Living Stones

St James', 1845

Living Stones

St James' Church, Kingston
1845–1995
From Stuartville to Queen's Campus

David Lyon

Canadian Cataloguing in Publication Data

Lyon, David, 1948–
   Living stones : St. James' Church, Kingston

Includes bibliographical references.
ISBN 1-55082-160-1
   1. St. James' Church (Kingston, Ont.)--History.
I. Title

BX5617.K5S34   1995   283'.71372   C95-900868-3

Design by Susan Hannah.

Printed and bound in Canada by
Best Book Manufacturers,
Toronto, Ontario.

Published by Quarry Press Inc.,
P.O. Box 1061, Kingston, Ontario.

"...you also, like living stones,
are being built into a spiritual house ..."
— 1 Peter 2:5

Contents

Preface & Acknowledgements

I can't recall exactly when it occurred to me that I could try to write the story of St James' for the sesquicentennial. All I know now is that it was already too late. There is far more material out there than I could manage to pull together in the time. Nonetheless, with the help and encouragement of people at St James' and elsewhere I have tried to weave the dominant threads into a story. From the start I wanted it to be, as far as possible, the people's story, not just that of rectors, still less something that bears heavy traces of my handiwork and prejudices. Of course, I'm responsible for the result, but I hope that many will recognise it as "their" story.

A project like this depends on the generosity, patience, ingenuity, sense of humour, forgiveness and love of many. It's hard to know where to begin to be fair to all. The person who's been involved longest and most deeply with the research process is Jenna Kennedy. Part of her contribution will become apparent as you read on. Other valued assistants, who collected stories, photos and so on included Marya Bootsma, Maggie Clark and Fiona Swift. Abi Lyon and Janet Henderson took photos. My secretary, Joan Westenhaefer, did a sterling job with draft preparation and guarding my research days.

Early and ongoing encouragement and advice came from Irene Cleland, Jane Sribney, Pat Patterson, Earle Thomas and Jack Henderson. Don Goertz and Ian Rennie gave guidance at the outset. Alan Hayes helped along the way, as did Marguerite van Die and George Rawlyk, who also kindly read the text for me. Others who commented were Bill Moore (more than once!), Jack Grenville, Shirley Spragge, Earle Thomas and Will Katerberg. People too numerous to mention gave me stories, anecdotes, contacts and leads. Librarians and archivists allowed us to pester them and other people cheerfully answered calls, letters and e-mail messages from a stranger. Those closest to me — Sue, Tim, Abi, Josh and Miriam — took an interest in my obsession well beyond the call of familial duty. I thank all.

The Social Science Research Council of Canada supported the research with a three year grant, and the Ontario Heritage Foundation contributed another grant towards publication. I am grateful to all. sdg

Foreword

It is not uncommon for Anglican churches to mark a special anniversary by writing the history of that particular parish. Usually such efforts are long on lists of clergy past and present, preoccupied with details of building construction and renovation, and frustratingly thin on analysis and interpretation of the underlying factors and influences which really shaped the life of that Christian community.

Professor David Lyon's fascinating story of St. James' Anglican Church, Kingston, is a refreshing contrast to most parish histories. Written to help St. James' celebrate its one hundred and fiftieth anniversary, it traces the story of this well-known parish from humble beginnings in a slum village adjacent to the town of Kingston, to a vibrant parish gathered in a Gothic limestone building on the edge of the Queen's University campus.

Living Stones is in the first instance a fascinating account of the clergy and lay people who worked in varying degrees of harmony to establish and maintain a congregation of faithful Anglican Christians. They were dedicated, strong, and varied individuals, with more than their share of spiritual conviction and outward fortitude. But they were also part of a series of larger movements and developments that shaped both the church and the social order across the nineteenth and twentieth centuries. Thus we are caught up in the con-

troversies of churchmanship which originated in England and Ireland in the mid nineteenth century, but spread across the ocean and took root in this country. We trace the growth of a church which welcomed merchants, soldiers, and entrepreneurs, and developed into a spiritual oasis for faculty and students of the nearby university. And we witness the ongoing tensions between the diocese and St. James', as the established church sought to impose its control upon the fledgling parish.

The history of St. James' is the story of people — clergy who usually remained in the position of rector for many years at a time, and lay people who contributed not just material support, but more importantly, enthusiastic leadership, faithful service, and occasionally spirited contentiousness. David Lyon skilfully brings them to life, and enables us to appreciate the effect each rector had on the welfare of the church, and how in turn each one's ministry flowed into that of his successor.

Of special interest is the degree of theological and spiritual consistency which endures in St. James' from its earliest years into the present. While certain more contentious aspects of evangelical Irish Protestantism have long been abandoned, a general spiritual ethos continues to inform the life of this particular church, usually because of, but occasionally in spite of one rector or another.

One hundred and fifty years have witnessed dramatic changes in Canadian Anglicanism. St. James' has not been spared these entirely; but it would be safe to say that despite social, economic, and religious upheavals, St. James' may be better situated than many other parishes not merely to survive well into the next century, but to prosper in fulfilling its mission to bear witness to the Christian message, and to serve those persons who are drawn and welcomed into its fellowship. All who love St. James', all who are interested in the religious history of Kingston, and all who are fascinated by the rise and progress of contemporary Canadian Christianity, will welcome and enjoy this book.

— *Peter Mason, Bishop of Ontario*

Introduction

Telling the story of a church is not as easy as it sounds, especially when the story covers more than one hundred and fifty years. A church building like St James', with its Ontario gothic limestone style, is easily recognised, a familiar landmark to any one who has spent any time in Kingston. But what do those old stones mean? What, far more significantly, has gone on in the lives of people who have worshipped there from generation to generation? And why was it not torn down long ago to make space for more laboratories and lecture-rooms for Queen's University?

A church, like a river, never stays the same. It may follow the same channel, so that you know it is the "same" river, but its composition, temperature, speed of flow and what it carries with it alters constantly. There are several strong senses in which St James' has remained the same. No one has tried to move the building, it is a Christian, Anglican church, and many of the prayers and hymns used in 1845 are still with us today. But along with this continuity has also come considerable change. The subtitle, *Stuartville to Queen's Campus,* says something about change.

The largest scale of change during St James' story can be summed up in one word, modernization. The city with which St James' life has been intertwined was a small but significant town in the 1840s, coping with the aftermath — psychological and economic — of its brief spell as capital of what is now Quebec and Ontario. Nearly all traffic was water-borne and thus communications came almost to a standstill in the ice-bound winter. Today, after numerous commercial and industrial experiments — of which some, like the locomotive shops, were quite successful for a time — Kingston is mainly a town of institutions; the prisons, higher education, health administration and so on. The presence of Alcan, Dupont and, further away, Celanese do not make Kingston an "industrial" city.

Many sociologists and historians writing about the churches and religion have assumed that modern means secular. Many older accounts suggest that the dreary statistics of declining attendance sound the death knell not only of churches but of religion itself. Today, the interpretive tide is starting to change and a more subtle story is being told, of falling here but rising there, of altered styles but persistent faith, even of less belonging, more believing. Where does St James' fit? Have the sleigh and streetcar, the telephone and television made a fatal difference? What about the relative contributions of women and men in the church; how have these changed with gender realignments? How has the church contributed to and been shaped by, such changes?

The second aspect of change is more peculiar to St James'. Not only have modernizing processes occurred in and around the church. Its immediate social surroundings have been transformed almost beyond recognition. The limestone building located first in an Irish immigrant slum now sits on the leafy campus of a leading Canadian university. This has significant implications for the church. The word "parish" that in its first hundred years had such strong geographical meaning is now reduced to mere metaphor. Almost.

The family-and-local-community orientation has given way to a mixed congregation; some walk from the student ghetto, others drive from out-of-town villages. Emerging town-gown relations are tested here. The challenge must constantly be faced of finding balance between the inevitable bias towards Queen's and other equally important aspects of church life. But from sharing the Queen's heating system to confronting the same social and intellectual issues, St James' cannot avoid having Queen's in her "parish," nor Queen's avoid having St James' on the campus.

Thirdly, like any organization, St James' has had different leaders. The story of the church is not the story of her leaders, but they are important, especially at St James', where rectors have remained on average more than eighteen years! Long-term leaders do tend to leave their mark on the congregation, so their life-stories are told in their own right at the ends of the main chapters. They yield some interesting insights into each

period. Lastly, there is the obvious point that historical data about them is often more available than for some other parishioners.

The three aspects of change mentioned above are of course affected by other factors, especially the fortunes of Christianity in Canada in general, the situation of Anglicans, and the relation between St James' and other churches in Kingston. Each of these elements is woven into the story, sometimes prominently part of the pattern, sometimes in more subdued tones. St James' is a microcosm of a bigger story of each of these three elements, while also telling its own distinctive tale.

So, how do continuity and change relate to each other? We still need some benchmark, some means of measuring the kinds of changes that have happened in the St James' story. In fact, the story itself offers one. The church was begun by a group of people who had clear vision, lots of energy, and the hopefulness of people, many of whom were starting afresh in a new land. The vision for a Christian life of worship and service that animated them would today be called "evangelical." So we can ask the question at each point, how far is this or that shift still faithful to the founding vision? Has the church become something significantly different from what it was in 1845?

For those who are interested in the future of the church as well as its past, this story also offers some clues. Memory can be connected with hope; how the church became what it is gives some guidance on how today's and tomorrow's issues might be faced. Certainly, nothing in the story that follows suggests that the church meeting on the Arch-Union corner is contemplating imminent closure.

Just a note on chronology. While a time line runs through the book — it begins in the 1840s and breaks off in the 1990s — in order to explore important themes I have also clustered material to some extent. I do not pretend to just tell the tale "like it was." So the story begins with a church in a relatively poor neighbourhood (chapter one), establishing itself as an evangelical congregation (chapter two). It is soon marked by its activism, seen especially in the temperance movement (chapter three) but this should not detract from all the ordinary day-to-day things happening in Stuartville and at St James' at the turn of the century (chapter four).

St James' also interacted with life well beyond Kingston, in the Canadian north and west, and in other countries, especially India and Japan (chapter five). It also felt the tensions of global events, world wars, yet these experiences mesh with mundane local social affairs (chapter six). The post-war boom years are also halcyon days for the churches, and Kingston churches are no exception. Indeed, the boom is accented at St James' (chapter seven). The pace of growth slows suddenly after the sixties (chapter eight) and the church is forced to ask serious questions about where it is going (chapter nine). Deterioration of the building by the nineties adds further urgency to those questions and I conclude by commenting on the trends and future options for the church (chapter ten).

The story of St James' is far from complete. Both in the sense that much more has happened than I have been able to relate, and in the sense that much has yet to happen, the story is ongoing. Its life spans several generations who have worshipped in the same building. But its secret lies neither in genealogy nor architecture, which is why I called the story *Living Stones*.

lisa's connection to stones as ancestors!?

1

Beginnings:
A Church for the Poor

You are my Irish grandfather:
. . . You were gone
before I knew enough to know
what to ask; and now all I have
is this photograph and a few memories
still current in the one blood
connection: your daughter, my mother.

— Bill Barnes[1]

A dozen ordinary people, none of them well-off, met in a nondescript schoolroom between William and Johnson Streets, Kingston on June 25, 1843.[2] They joined in Christian worship, following the prayer book of the United Church of England and Ireland, and sang, we believe, to the music of John Cooper's 'cello. Robert Rogers, newly returned to Kingston as penitentiary chaplain after a convalescent visit to England, led the meeting and preached. His sermon was based directly on a biblical text. No doubt before they parted they discussed their plans for meeting again, and how they would publicise the event to others. Thus began the church that would become St James'.

The dozen people included Robert Rogers' wife Mary; a brewer, Micah Mason; and a soldier; plus, perhaps, Thomas Wade, later to be sexton.[3] The room where they met was in the "Line Barracks" School, no doubt attended by children of soldiers.[4] At forty, Rogers would easily have been the oldest present. They were mainly Irish immigrants, though Rogers himself was English. They were starting life together in the New World, seeking new opportunities and fresh freedom for their religion. St George's, the only Anglican[5] church in town, was packed to overflowing by the recent arrivals. As well, some newcomers felt slightly uneasy there. A hint of disapproval hung in the air. Seeking a more congenial alternative seemed like an obvious move.

Rogers was in Kingston as a missionary of the Society for the Propagation of the Gospel (SPG), on an income cobbled together from them, from teaching at the Midland District school and from the penitentiary. But his decade of North American experience and the fact that he was well-liked by the Irish Protestants among whom he had worked in Richmond recommended Rogers to the group meeting in the schoolroom. He would have been aware already of their independent spirit and their suspicion of religious elites.

Although good reasons existed for starting a new congregation, it could also be seen by fellow Anglicans as breakaway group. The hint of disapproval at St George's probably reflected some snobbery about the prospects for a church starting in a very humble schoolroom, doubts about what could happen if these Irish hotheads were given free rein, and also caution about the evangelical convictions of the fledgling church.

What was happening in Kingston reflected some broader tensions, about the place of evangelical "enthusiasm" within the United Church of England and Ireland and the role of that church in the New World. These twin tensions were to be formative for St James'.

Anglicans had tended to look over their shoulders to England as they contemplated taming and civilizing the Canadian wilderness. Lieutenant-Governor John Graves Simcoe, for instance, sought an established church for Upper Canada, that would be supported by income from land — the "clergy reserves," being one seventh of crown lands in the colony — and that would in turn buttress a political system of social hierarchy headed by the king. But it was an unrealistic dream, both because of the relatively small number of Anglican clergy at the turn of the century and because many Upper Canadians were already North Americans who had moved from neighbouring New York and the eastern seaboard.[6] The established church idea would not last.

The other tension was between mainstream Anglicanism and groups affected by revival, on the one hand, and by a desire to restore the purity of the reformational church of Archbishop Cranmer, on the other. Evangelical awakening began on both sides of the Atlantic in the early eighteenth century, when people such as John Wesley found themselves drawn to God in a new and personal way, and renewed churches began to spread this influence in both missionary outreach and social activism.

Robert Rogers was evidently affected by this

church & panel connection!

The Midland District Schoolroom, where the pre-St James'
congregation met, appears on the left of this view west on King
Street by Mrs. Cartwright, c. 1835. More building would have
appeared by 1843 (Queen's University Archives, QUA).

movement. But because those comprising the
main part of the early St James' congregation were
Irish, the perceived "problem" of Roman
Catholicism was also high on the agenda. For
Irish evangelicals, more than for English, this system of religious error had to be opposed so that
the gospel of Jesus could shine through clearly.[7]

One could be forgiven for seeing in the first
gathering in the Line Barracks schoolroom some
resemblance to the New Testament church. St
James' began with twelve mainly poor people,
meeting in a very plain room, on a dusty, unmade
street, and with less than full approval of the local
religious establishment. Like that first century
church, they were driven by a strong sense of mission. And again, like their earlier counterparts,
they would soon be charged, if not with turning
the world upside down, at least with trying to be
different, upsetting the *status quo*.

Like the early church, St James' people saw
themselves as starting over, in a rapidly growing
community. But like the early church, these people also came into a new context with their own
histories. The result of this mix was a church that
forged a fresh path forward, within what would
become a distinctively Canadian evangelical
Anglicanism.

THE IRISH AND THE NEW CHURCH

The early 1840s were exciting, busy and turbulent times in Kingston. The town was growing
rapidly as waves of largely Irish immigrants settled

The Kingston General Hospital as it appeared in the 1840s.
St James' congregation met here when it was still known as
the parliament building.

At this time, indeed throughout the nineteenth century, the Irish formed the largest ethnic group in British North America. Before and after the Great Famine of 1846-49, Protestant Irish immigrants to Upper Canada outnumbered their Catholic cousins 2:1, and most came from north-central Ireland. They came for a chance to start afresh, not just because they were dirt poor.[8] Having said that, the poorest settlers in Kingston were Irish, and they were most highly concentrated in Stuartville, the area where most of the new congregation lived.

The population of Kingston in 1841 was 8,400, plus more than 3000 in the "suburbs." Immigrant labour was involved in the building projects that abounded at that time, including City Hall, St Mary's Cathedral, four Martello Towers and the Market battery. Upper and Lower Canada had just been united and redesignated Canada East and Canada West, under Governor General Lord Sydenham's initiative. The same year, 1841, a Board of Trade was organized in Kingston, the Parliament of Canada met here for the first time, and Queen's University received its Royal Charter. By 1843, Kingston lawyer John A Macdonald was elected alderman, and the following year, MP. And only a few years previously, the Kingston Penitentiary was built (1836) and Kingston became a city (1838), with Thomas Kirkpatrick as its first mayor.

The group that would form St James' Church met regularly from 1843, first in the Line Barracks School Room, afterwards in the Midland District School on King Street. The story is often told that Anthony O'Loughlin, a cabinet-maker in his mid-twenties, then invited them to use his furniture store at Brock and Clergy. According to his family history, however, he had yet to arrive in Kingston. Of course, the church may have met in a furniture store, but there is no record whose, or where it was.[9] Later they met in the Parliament Buildings, recently vacated by the move of the seat of government to Montreal, and soon to become part of Kingston General Hospital.

In 1844 the Honourable John Macaulay gave land for a church building "for the convenience of the working classes" at Arch and Union — then a cow pasture track — and a cornerstone on this "Lot 24" was laid by John Strachan, Bishop of Toronto, on September 28. The building committee, which included Kirkpatrick the mayor,[10] chose William Coverdale as architect — he designed many other well-known Kingston buildings — and oversaw the rapid completion of the building ready for its opening service one year later. The building cost a little over 800 pounds and was paid for by private subscription among Kingston citizens. Many workers also volunteered their labour.

The church building told its own story. Forsaking the classical lines of St George's, it conformed to the new rules of "Ontario gothic."[11] This both harked back, romantically, to the medieval church, but also reached forward to the future reign of the transcendent God whose majesty was suggested by its architectural lines.

J. LINTON

Kingston, September 6, 1844. 20z

NOTICE.

TENDERS for the Erection of a Church in Union-street, Lot 24, according to Plans and Specifications lying at the Store of Mr. Brent, Chemist, will be received on or before Wednesday, September 18th instant, by

R. V. ROGERS,
Sec. Building Com.

Kingston, September 3, 1844. 19

FIRE BRICK for sale by
H. & O.

Notice appearing in the *Kingston Chronicle and Gazette*, September 11, 1844.

Carpenters, masons, painters and labourers volunteered their services to help build St James' in 1844.

TO THE
INHABITANTS OF STUARTVILLE,
MEMBERS OF THE CHURCH OF ENGLAND, AND OTHERS.

DEAR BRETHREN:

WITH GOD'S PERMISSION, DIVINE SERVICE will be on Sundays at a quarter past 11, A.M., and half-past 6 o'clock, P.M.

THE LORD'S SUPPER will be administered on the second Sunday in every Month. Persons desirous of communicating for the first time are requested to inform me of it at least a week previously, so that an opportunity may be afforded for instruction, &c. &c.

BAPTISM will be administered, publicly, on the first Sunday in every month. You are requested to be as particular as possible in your selection of Sponsors. Sponsors should be careful to respond in the words of the Service, and not to be satisfied with giving silent consent.

PRIVATE BAPTISM will not be administered, *except in case of illness.*

MARRIAGES will be solemnized in the Church.

FUNERALS.—Except on very special occasions, the Clergyman will meet the corpse either at the entrance of the Church, or the Grave-yard.

When the tax of time and strength is considered, neither of which the Congregation can impose without injury to themselves as well as their Minister, it is hoped that the motive which has led to this departure from the custom of this place will be fully appreciated by a returning to the ancient mode.

CATECHIZING—*One day* in each week, at different points, so as best to suit the convenience of the members. The day, and hour, and place, will be given out on the previous Lord's Day.

It is requested that all who have the charge of Children will, to their utmost, aid their Minister in this department of his labors.

SUNDAY SCHOOL from 9 to 11 o'clock, A.M. Parents are requested to see that their Children are punctual in attendance, and aid the Teachers in every way. Persons desirous of acting as Teachers are requested to inform the Minister or Superintendent.

THE CHOIR will meet for practice once every week.

Persons wishing to assist in this part of Divine Worship will signify the same to the Leader of the Choir, who will communicate with the Minister: their names will, if approved, be enrolled; when it will be their object to promote the glory of God by singing to His praise.

Two Day Schools are in operation under the patronage of this Church: the one at Portsmouth, Miss Bryant, Teacher; the other in Stuartville, Mrs Hornby, Teacher. These Schools are regularly visited by the Clergyman, where *free* instruction will be given to those who are not able to pay for it.

In presenting the above to your friendly consideration, may I take the opportunity of requesting your co-operation both by prayer and best exertions, that your Pastor may be a workman that needeth not to be ashamed, and the flock committed to his charge grow in grace and in the knowledge of their God and Savior, "till we all come in the unity of the faith, and knowledge of the Son of God, unto a perfect man, unto the measure of the stature of the fulness of Christ."

Often meditate on such passages as these: Ephes. iv. c., 1 Thess. v., 2 Pet. iii. 18.

A Box will be placed in the Church to receive every Sunday that portion of your worldly substance which you can spare, 1st, for your poor brethren, and 2d, the support of the Church. See 1 Cor. xvi. verses 1, 2.

Believe me,
Your Servant for Christ's sake,
R. V. ROGERS, *Minister.*

BY permission of the Worshipful the Mayor and Corporation of Kingston,

A BAZAAR

is proposed to be held in the Town Hall the first week in August, in order to raise funds for completing the interior fittings of St. James's Church, Stuartville, (Lot 24.)

Any contributions for promoting this object will be thankfully received by those Ladies of the Committee who have kindly consented to hold tables, whose names are subjoined.

Hon. MRS. DEBLAQUIERE,
MRS. CASSIDY,
MRS. SADLIER,
MRS. DUPUY,
MRS. BRENT,
MRS. R. V. ROGERS.

Editors friendly to the above object are requested to give this an insertion.

St James' first church bazaar, organized by women in 1845 (*Kingston Chronicle and Gazette* May 28).

The earliest photo of St James',
c. 1850 (Diocese of Ontario Archives, DOA).

St James', c. 1850. Note the boardwalks and the two
children who ran off while the frame was being exposed!
(DOA).

But at least two features lent it a peculiarly Protestant character. The lack of a basement kept the walls low, earthbound, reinforcing the sense that it was not just a church for the socially elevated. And the lack of a chancel meant that the main sanctuary was a simple rectangular room with no separate spaces for "priest and people."[12]

Rogers' notice, advertising the start of services to the "inhabitants of Stuartville," also mentioned the existence of a choir and a Sunday School (that already had 60 scholars) plus two day schools (one in Stuartville and the other in Portsmouth) all under the aegis of the infant church. Baptisms, marriages and funerals had been conducted since 1844. By the time the church began to meet in the new building the 'cellist had been joined by two violinists and a cornet-player. The church bought a melodeon in 1848.

The building was formally opened with a service on September 24 1845, led by Robert Rogers and the Rev. W. Dawes, at which William Herchmer preached on Genesis 28:16: "The Lord is in this place . . . ." George Okill Stuart of St George's was present and the mood was celebratory. No doubt poorer people were there in some force; two-thirds of the sittings were free from the start. That is, people could attend without paying pew rents if they lacked the means. Exactly how bills were to be paid would be a matter of controversy for some time to come. At that first service, however, the main sentiment was gratitude for a new place to worship, that had been built with such tremendous speed.

Within four years of completing the church building a parsonage was also constructed, which for many years was the only one in Kingston attached to an Anglican church. Built by subscription, the parsonage — today, "rectory" — faced the courthouse on the corner of Barrie and Union Streets. One of the subscribers, incidentally, was one John A. Macdonald, who contributed five pounds.

Unfortunately, each spring, the parsonage cellar flooded, making it necessary to get into a tub to reach the stored food! At the back of the house stood a large stone shed where ashes from the church and parsonage stoves were put before their removal by a man who made soap from them. Beside the shed, cordwood was stored for both buildings, and behind it was a thicket of wild plum trees. Within a few years a vegetable garden appeared, along with a cow and a flock of hens, kept in by twelve-foot-high pointed slats.[14]

WHY THE CHURCH BEGAN

Why did St James' begin at this particular point in time? Undoubtedly, first, a large part of the initiative came from an early chapter of what was to become the Church Society.[15] They provided for travelling missionaries, and provided Bibles, Christian books and tracts to sell to passengers arriving at Kingston docks, as well as encouraging church extension through providing buildings and support for clergy.[15]

The role of the choir: Robert Rogers concurred with Micah Mason who ". . . viewed praise as an essential part of the worship of Almighty God, and considered the choir as the leader and assistant of the congregation and not as forming a distinct office for a duty which it alone should discharge; and with which it is presumptuous for other worshippers to interfere."[13]

Part of the 1849 subscription list to build the St James' parsonage. Many of the names are well-known.

The Church Society was incorporated in 1842, in Toronto, in response to a funding crisis sparked externally by a cut in grants from Britain in 1831 and internally by disputes over the revenue from clergy reserves.[16] The latter guaranteed church income from landholdings, especially for Anglicans. At a time of rapid immigration the cuts were bad news indeed. But the Church Society did not come into being without controversy.[17]

Recognising that if support for the young church could not be expected from its traditional English source, the state, it would have to come from lay people, the Church Society was actually controlled by a "Lay Committee." This level of democratic involvement bothered those from the more upper class, establishment end of Anglicanism, who felt more comfortable with rule by a clerical elite. The Church Society scheme lasted until the creation of diocesan synods in the 1850s, which drew on a wider base of support.

The Church Society responded, secondly, to the obvious need for churches to serve the growing population, a fourth of which was Church of England and Ireland (the name it kept until it reverted to the Church of England in 1871). In 1848 the population of Stuartville (then outside Kingston) stood at 2,286, and each immigrant ship added to their number.[18] Within four years, three other Anglican churches were built to cope with the influx; St Paul's and St John's Kingston and St Mark's, Barriefield.[19] St James' was intended to serve not only Stuartville but also Hatter's Bay, later known as Portsmouth.

The parsonage, as it appeared in an 1850s water-
colour (whose whereabouts are now unknown).
Note that this is before the porch and rear
extensions were added.

But from the start there was also, thirdly, some distancing from St George's. George Okill Stuart, the rector, announced that St James' would be a "free" church, that is, responsible for its own welfare. Although neither Rogers nor Stuart were of "high church" persuasion, controversy between St James' and St George's broke out not many years later.

Rogers was evangelical. He relied more on the Bible than on tradition and held that conversion to Christ was required rather then just being part of a church. One suspects that the "odium" with which the young congregation was viewed sprang not only from their "common" meeting place, as Rogers hinted, but from some differences of opinion already making themselves felt. By this time Rogers' evangelicalism was becoming well-known in Upper Canada.

Lastly, the new congregation had the advantage of an energetic and experienced leader in Rogers. He came with a sense of mission, both to serve a community that was largely poor and whose social and cultural roots in Upper Canada were as yet only shallow, and to do so with a robustly biblical approach that placed scripture above tradition and ecclesiastical precedent. He was a leading figure in what was sometimes called the "evangelical party", with little time for religious elitism or wistfulness for the privileges of English clergy.[20] While not denying "rank," still less loyalty to the crown, he encouraged lay activity in the church, lay support for the church, and saw St James' as a strategic base from which he could help develop a new kind of Anglicanism in a new country. Such a stance would also, of course, spark opposition.

THE CHURCH IN A SLUM

The Reverend John Stuart, a reluctant loyalist, was Kingston's first Anglican rector. He was a gifted and faithful minister. He owned Lot 24, that became known as "Stuartville." While the maps show this clearly enough, popular usage of "Stuartville" included more and less than the map. It could be from Barrie to University and from the Lake to 1st Concession, but more commonly Stuartville was thought of as the area immediately north of union to Johnson between Barrie and the farmland west beyond Division.

Stuart's son, who would give his name to five streets — Arch, Deacon, George, Okill, and Stuart — took over the land and "developed" it. He has become at least as well known, perhaps unfairly, for his efforts at property development as for his spiritual stature. Although he consistently supported many good causes with both time and money, it is hard to resist the conclusion that he also created "Stuart's slum."[21] During all the early years of St James, Stuartville was the centre of hot political controversy.

In the 1830s and 1840s many Kingstonians saw Stuartville as a "nightmare" that would haunt Kingston and give it a reputation as a "miserable village" until something was done to clean it up. It was crowded, unsanitary, and "copiously dotted with hogpens and slaughterhouses and consequent accumulations of feculent matter."[22] The mainly Irish population, many of whom were unmarried male labourers, plus widows and orphans, often lived from hand-to-mouth as tenants in frame and clapboard houses, frequenting the numerous taverns available in the vicinity.

They were vulnerable to cholera and typhus, which struck ghastly blows, especially in 1832, 1834 and 1847. On the last occasion, 1,200 immigrants were buried in a common grave. The only relief from slum life appeared in the houses of the rich — like Stuart's own Summerhill — which were built with lake views. Little surprise that Stuartville was viewed as a "crying evil" by the inhabitants of Kingston.

The controversy centred on whether or not Stuartville should be incorporated within Kingston. The poorer people who sought lodging in Stuartville did so because rents were low and because, being outside town, they could evade police tax. The town of Kingston, on the other hand, wished to widen the tax base in order to pay off the large debt incurred in building a City Hall dignified enough for a capital city. Needless to say, Stuart opposed incorporation. Eventually however, under the Municipal Act of 1849, Kingston used its new powers to annex Stuartville in 1850, thus ending more than a decade of political wrangling.

The "labourers and mechanics" who lived in Stuartville found employment in the numerous construction projects from fortifications to the Napanee road. Many were employed at the new penitentiary and the docks. Unskilled labourers, mariners and penitentiary guards comprised a part of St James' first congregation, but there were also ship's carpenters, shoemakers, a butcher, a candlemaker, a chandler, a blacksmith, a clerk, an upholsterer and so on. Among higher status occupations were a schooner captain, an army quartermaster, a school teacher, a medical doctor and a lawyer, Thomas Kirkpatrick, who would become mayor again in 1847.[23]

When Robert Rogers began meeting with the embryonic St James' congregation, as chaplain he would have seen other parishioners who worked at the penitentiary, and would also have seen parents of children under his care at the Midland District School. It is clear from his previous experience as a travelling missionary and from the references in sermons to the ordinary people of the congregation that his heart would have been with the disadvantaged people of Stuartville from the start. Whether the disadvantage was religious, racial or economic, Rogers was their champion. He was used to contending for the underdog.[24]

The chief reason he had come to Canada was the difficulty of maintaining his anti-slavery convictions in Ohio. Once in Kingston, he continued to work for ordinary people. He held services in the County Jail, (behind the courthouse) and in the General Hospital. And he requested that his congregation give their weekly offerings "1st, for your poor brethren, and 2nd, the support of the

Clean up the city: go to church!
If "cleanliness is next to godliness" as I have heard remarked, the inhabitants of Lot 24 need not trouble themselves about building another Church for some time, for if the maxim is correct the one they are now building will be more than sufficient for ten times their number, if the hearers are to be only such as set upon that fine aphorism, and as the same is equally applicable to many of the Town's folk, such of them as may think the cap suits them are perfectly welcome to wear it.

Letter to the Editor Kingston Chronicle and Gazette *on "Kingston nuisances" May 10 1845.*

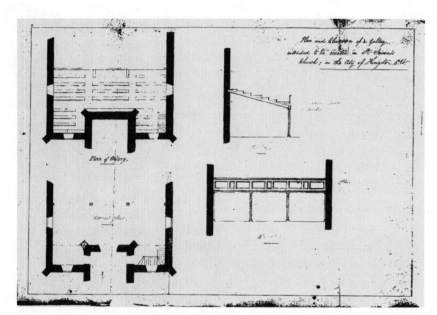

Plans for the gallery (built 1855) that
would later be demolished (1926).

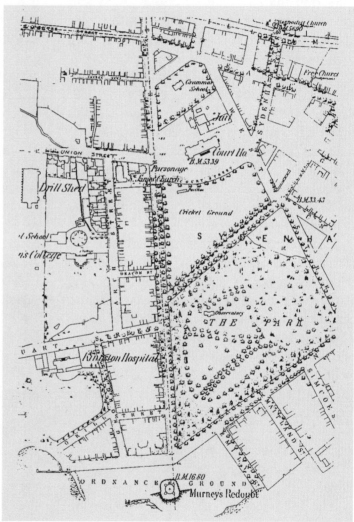

An 1868 plan of the
Stuartville area (QUA).

church."[25] Even though the church grew fast — the congregation numbered 400 with 110 in "Sabbath School" in 1849[26] — this did not necessarily mean they were more comfortably off.

When in 1855 the church wished to add a gallery to accommodate more (poor) people, Rogers wrote asking for support from friends in England. He reminded them that the church had been started for the "poorer classes" and that they had "increased in number but not in wealth." That relative poverty continued to characterise much of the congregation well into the century is also evident from Francis Kirkpatrick Jnr's memory that in 1880 "a considerable part [of the open collection] was in coppers."

Slums did not remain in Stuartville for all that long, however. After Stuartville was annexed into Kingston, things began to improve. Local businesses began to spring up. During the later 1850s and 1860s many of the rough wooden homes were replaced by brick and stone dwellings. Families were raised and the population stabilized. Households contained on average five people, though families of ten plus were not uncommon. Employment opportunities expanded, although there was still not enough work for available labour. And the proportion of unskilled jobs in Stuartville fell from 55% to 29% between 1861-1871.

The Irish still predominated, though the proportion of Catholics fell and some Scottish Presbyterians were also added. In 1861, 45% Stuartville households were "Anglican" (used here as shorthand for the United Church of England and Ireland), 25% RC, 22% English and Scots Presbyterians plus a few Methodists and Congregationalists (though the Methodists would grow rapidly in the following decade).[27] While St James' contacts with the Catholics would be cautious, and, as we shall see, occasionally caustic, contact with other churches was cordial and cooperative.

This, then, was the setting for the start of a new church. It was peopled mainly by new settlers who brought with them their vigorous Irish Protestant convictions. It was led by a man of equally strong views, biblically based, and tempered by a concern for the disadvantaged. Both lay-people and leader believed that much was at stake for the future of the church in Upper Canada. They were determined that the church should make its mark and play its part, in Stuartville, in Kingston, and well beyond.

PROFILE

ROBERT ROGERS (1803–1886)
RECTOR 1843–1869

St James' church owed much to the vision and energy of its first leader, Robert Vashon Rogers. Despite ill-health and opposition he shepherded the young congregation until, a quarter of a century later, it was a thriving community at the centre of the life of Stuartville.

Born at St George's, near Pill, Somerset, England in 1803, Rogers was the second son of a navy captain, John Fowler Rogers. Only seven years old when his father died, Robert was cared for by a guardian who was also his private tutor, Dr Andrew Jackson, Dean of Christ Church College, Oxford. What happened next is unclear. One source states that on starting his studies at Cambridge University he intended to become a lawyer, but soon switched to theology. But while other records of his life are good, they are simply missing at this point.

If Rogers was at Cambridge then it would have been in the years when Charles Simeon was in his prime as Vicar of Holy Trinity. Simeon was also a fellow of King's College, and had a great impact on students, many of whom came to evangelical convictions under his influence.[28] He had a vision of Christian commitment at the heart of the university. Moreover Simeon often sent young men to the British colonies, not just as chaplains to immigrants, but to minister to native peoples. Rogers was to go in such a way, but whether or not this was because of Simeon, we do not know. However, it *is* clear that Rogers' sermons would soon show the same high view of the Bible that characterised Simeon's ministry. It would be surprising if there were no connection.

Politically, anti-slavery was the great cause that caught the imagination of evangelicals at this time, and led to alliances with others of like mind. William Wilberforce, the anti-slave campaigner, was a close friend of Simeon. The so-called "Clapham Sect," which, among other things, fought slavery, represented the kind of evangelical activism that would be espoused by Rogers. Although Wilberforce's bill to abolish slave trading was passed in 1807, the struggle was to continue throughout the century, and this too had an impact on the young Rogers. Indeed, it became the reason he wound up in Canada.

We do know that Rogers was ordained deacon, to be a curate at Hessle Parish Church in Yorkshire in 1827. The same year he married Mary Best Howells. Three years later, in response to a call from Bishop Chase of Ohio for people to be involved in missions, they sailed for the New World.[29]

Although Rogers was offered the chance to join the faculty of a new theological college, because of some potential conflicts there[30] he opted for service as a travelling missionary. He was based first in Worthington, Ohio, with the Episcopal Church. As it turned out, this was not an easy charge. Travelling proved arduous, and may in time have affected his health. As his next employer, Bishop Stewart, would put it, these were the "days of corduroy and the saddle, and weary journeyings and scant comfort."[31] During these years he once took a vacation in the Canadas, when recovering from a cholera attack.

But the bigger burden than the trials of travel was slavery, still a very sore spot in the Ohio of the 1830s. Eventually a "sense of duty" — his anti-slavery convictions — led him to resign, and the decision was reluctantly accepted by the wardens and vestry of St Philip's, Circleville OH in 1836. The anti-slavery work was to surface again in Canada, although, ironically, it was not uncontroversial there either.

Meanwhile Bishop Stewart of Quebec requested that he go to Kingston via Toronto, en route for the "Richmond Mission, between Perth and Bytown" (Ottawa). The locals (including the Orange Order!) were delighted to have this energetic young man serve in their church and were disappointed when ill-health forced him to resign after only three years. John Strachan, bishop of Toronto intervened this time, proposing a sideways move for Rogers, to replace William MacCaulay Herchmer as chaplain to the new penitentiary in Kingston and to teach as headmaster of the Midland District School.

Thus Rogers arrived in Kingston in October

Rev. Robert Rogers
c. 1869.

1839, where he stayed for two years. As penitentiary chaplain he made it clear that he saw character reform and not mere punitive measures as the purpose of incarceration: ". . . it should ever be remembered, the safe keeping of the convict is not the end proposed, but his safe keeping in order that certain means may be adapted for his moral transformation."[32] This position was significant in Kingston where a scandal over prison brutality occurred in the late 1840s.

No doubt it was during this two year sojourn in Kingston that he built up the circle of friends from St George's who would eventually join the new cause in Stuartville. After a brief spell of renewed missionary travelling based at the Carrying Place his health broke again, this time with typhoid. He and Mary returned to England at this point, and during his convalescence he acted as curate at Droxford in the Winchester diocese.

The pull of Canada came next through the Society for the Propagation of the Gospel, who sent him back as a missionary in 1843. Under its aegis he began organizing a congregation in Kingston's western suburbs, beyond the land Henry Murney once thought would be the grounds of the parliament (now City Park) and in Hatter's Bay (now Portsmouth). In this year their son was born, Robert Vashon junior. It was an appropriate time for the Rogers family to be settled in one place.

From this point, Rogers' story intersects fully with that of St James'. He provided leadership for the church by his personal example and within his family, and also through his consistent teaching. His sermons were always Bible-based, as he tried to expound the meaning of the text and to apply it to his hearers. Every occasion was treated in the same way. When his trusted friend and co-founder Micah Mason died, for instance, Rogers compared him with the New Testament character Barnabas, using for his points the text, "a good man, full of the Holy Ghost and of faith."[33]

Rogers was neither a bookish intellectual nor a developer of real estate. He had a heart for the people and a missionary spirit. In introducing himself to the new congregation he requested their "cooperation both by prayer and best exertions, that your Pastor may be a workman that needeth not be ashamed, and the flock committed to his charge grow in grace and the knowledge of their God and Savior . . ."[34] As it turned out, the gentle pastor could also be a fiery Protestant on occasion. After being at St James' twenty years he asked that friends "charge it to [his] account" if they had found him "unnecessarily severe." After all, he reflected, "Men who feel deeply cannot always speak gently."[35]

His concern for Irish immigrants, the group that predominated in Stuartville, was evident to all, through his teaching at Midland District, through the free gallery seating in the church building and so on. He also remained committed to the anti-slavery cause. Although many other Anglicans were indifferent to or at least not outspoken on the issue, evangelicals like Rogers — and his counterpart at Little Trinity, Toronto, Alexander Sanson — were well known for their involvement as out-and-out abolitionists. Though Kingston was not a "station" on the "underground railway," Rogers served on the board of the newly-formed Anti-Slavery Society of Canada from 1852.[35]

Given Rogers' anti-slavery views it would not be surprising if he had penned the following words, that appeared in the Kingston Argus in 1851: "That the inhabitants of Canada can sit still and look upon this struggle going on in the neighbouring republic is utterly impossible... Every town and city along the line which boasts of a dozen Christians should have its branch anti-slavery society forming so many harbours of refuge where the weary and hunted fugitives may find protection from the human bloodhounds who pursue them."[37]

Rogers was ever the indefatigable champion of the evangelical cause in Upper Canada. He often travelled to other places, not only for the anti-slavery work, but also in connection with magazine agencies. *The Church*, with its "high" views and its leanings to Rome — as the evangelicals saw it — could not satisfactorily represent the views of all, so an alternative was sought.

The Berean began in Quebec in the 1840s, and Rogers was the local agent in Kingston. Some of his sermons were printed in it. When that folded in 1849, Upper Canadian evangelicals started *The Echo and Protestant Episcopal Recorder*, published in Port Hope. Rogers was on the editorial committee and was again an agent. St James' churchwarden, P.B. de Blaquiere was also involved.[38] Major controversies over the alleged ritualistic tendencies of the Anglican college in Cobourg and over who might become bishop in Kingston, were fought out between *The Church* and *The Echo*.

In 1847, the congregation had persuaded Rogers that for his health's sake he should resign from the penitentiary although he continued to hold services in the County Jail and the General Hospital. He was also involved in projects such as starting the YMCA in Kingston. In 1856 Rogers received an honorary MA from the Archbishop of Canterbury and in 1860 he was appointed rural dean. In 1863, in recognition of twenty years service to the congregation and in Kingston, parishioners, plus members of other churches, gave him a handsome gift of $141.00 — "some slight expression of the esteem which they entertain for you" and a heartfelt letter of thanks.

He finally resigned from St James' in 1869. Not only did his own congregation give him the warmest of thanks, he also received testimonials — leaving gifts — from members of several other local churches, including St Andrew's, Chalmers, Brock Street Presbyterian, the Wesleyan Methodists, Primitive Methodists and Congregationalists. He was clearly a well-known

Robert Vashon Rogers in his later years (c. 1880) DOA.

and well-loved Christian leader well beyond the confines of his own denomination.

So at age 66 he moved to the diocese of Huron, to work for the mission to Vittoria and, eventually, to oversee the erection of a church building at Port Ryerse. He was then briefly at Port Stanley, 1871–73. Rogers returned to Kingston where he stayed until his death in 1886. He was still leading an adult Bible class at the hospital at age eighty! His work for the parish is celebrated in the space named for him, the "Rogers Room" which began as the church hall and was subsequently renovated as a chapel. It reverted to being a room for social activities in the 1950s.

Grace Clara O'Loughlin, daughter of the cabinet-maker, recalls attending St James' as a child in the 1850s: "Mother would put the younger members down to sit on the kneeling bench and refresh the inner man by eating a cracker. I am afraid we were not the best behaved during the church service as we were quite amused by the reflection of Dr Rogers' nose on the wall, he having been blessed with an unusually long one."

Another Grace O'Loughlin reminiscence concerns ". . . my younger brother Mac at about 12 years old attending evening service at St James' Church. He had been sitting in the gallery and had fallen asleep. Nobody wakened him when church was over and consequently he was left in the building alone and the sexton put out the lights and locked up. He finally awoke and found himself alone and in the dark and came down to the door where he made such a racket and a row that the sexton, who lived just across the street, came over and unlocked the door and released the lad. When he came home he found that the whole neighbourhood had been out looking for him — and the lost sheep had returned."[39]

2

An Evangelical Identity

"The whole congregation looked towards them.
Then each member turned to his neighbour
and whispered the word 'Papist'."

— Jane Urquhart[1]

From the start, St James' was a church with clear viewpoints and strongly held convictions. One incident has taken on almost legendary significance: the sermon in a surplice. In 1855, a clergyman by the name of Saltern Givins had the temerity to preach at a St James' confirmation service, wearing both surplice — a white linen outer vestment — and gown.[2] The ensuing controversy led to a vestry resolution — proposed by John Comer — that this was "highly improper" and "determined that a repetition . . . shall not be made."[3] In fact, the surplice controversy would surface several times.[4]

One March night in 1863, for instance, when Robert Rogers arrived at the new St George's Cathedral to give a Lent lecture on "Scripture as a means of grace," the young bishop John Travers Lewis refused to let him preach without wearing a surplice. Determined to gain control over what he saw as the inappropriate autonomy of Kingston churchpeople, Lewis stood his ground. The bishop had recently — and controversially[5] — appointed likeminded William Lauder to replace George Okill Stuart as rector of Kingston. In the vestry Lewis asked Lauder if he "had a sermon in his pocket." "Yes, my Lord," came the reply. "That will do very well," said the bishop, walking out of the vestry without a word to Rogers.[6]

From the vantage point of the late twentieth

The Rev. Saltern Givens, whose wearing of the surplice to preach at St James' sparked major controversy (*History of the County of Lennox and Addington*, Belleville 1972).

century, what a minister wears in the pulpit may seem a pretty trivial concern. Why waste time and energy on matters so small? In the mid-nineteenth century, the surplice was a symbol of sympathy with "ritualism." For evangelical members of the United Church of England and Ireland, this was one of several symbols whose use would signal a perceived drift from the "truth" and towards Roman Catholicism. Seen this way, however, it would be easy to write off incidents like this as examples of a now outgrown bigotry or intolerance — on either side — between so-called "high" and "low" church factions in early Ontario.

Whatever we may now make of the surplice incidents, it is important to explore more fully their meaning, not only for St James' and Kingston, but also their place in the story of Canadian Christianity in general. The symbolic battles, over surplices, sung services, credence tables, candles and so on, highlight several features of Victorian church life in Ontario. One is that biblical truth was believed to be at stake, and there was a strong desire that "pure religion" would flourish in the New World. Another is that these were no clerical squabbles taking place in isolated cloisters. Laypeople were deeply and centrally involved, and the controversies were reported and reprinted in the press.

Beyond these factors, however, the clashes taking place in Kingston would help shape the future direction of Canadian Christianity. While

Anglican ecclesiastics did sometimes win the day over local congregations, those congregations also formed powerful and lasting alliances with other like-minded churches. Anti-Catholicism was one formative factor in what would later become evangelical identity. St James' was part of a broadly evangelical transdenominational movement that, by the end of the century, had achieved a position of cultural leadership in Ontario.

So the "sermon in the surplice" tells quite a tale. Whether a sermon was preached with or without the surplice being worn indicated the religious inclinations of the preacher. But there is also much to be learned from these incidents about the nature of Christianity in Kingston, and in Canada. Those who refused the surplice did not seem to be conflict-mongers or blind bigots but people conscientiously committed to a greater cause. They may well have exaggerated the extent of the "papist threat." But they wanted biblical Christianity to shine through both doctrine and practice. So Robert Rogers could say that when he held to Anglican standards, it was only ". . . from believing their consistency with the Word of God."[7]

A SENSE OF DIRECTION

The young church that met in Stuartville had a clear sense of direction. Members were not only drawn from the same area in the city — and many could also identify with life in faraway Ireland — but they also knew what they stood for in religious terms. The firm Protestant convictions of the rector were shared by the congregation. It is clear that their primary commitment was to the cause of Christ, expressed, naturally enough, in the context and culture of their day.

Week by week the church met in the building whose timbers still smelled fresh, warmed in the summer by the sun on the roof and in the winter by the crackle of blazing logs in the two iron stoves. The worshippers followed the simple Prayer Book forms, sang hymns with some gusto, led now by 'cello, violin and cornet, and listened to carefully crafted sermons, usually from Robert Rogers. The craft of these sermons was not so much literary as biblical, though Rogers did not lack the gift of eloquence.

Rogers and his flock believed in the Bible. Not only did they believe it to be true, they believed that it was the only sure route to finding the Jesus of history as the focus for faith. Moreover, they claimed that the Bible's teaching was superior to the authority of church traditions, and that following its principles of morality was the best basis possible for social life. Hardly surprising, then, that the Bible featured so prominently in the gatherings of the church.

When Rogers climbed into the pulpit, then on the East side of the sanctuary, he took with him his Bible and, one suspects, copious notes. The sermons were sometimes reproduced in print, and they show both attention to detail and a desire to relate faith to daily life. Sermons were always Bible-based, not as springboard but as structure. The text was not used as an excuse to air personal opinions or to purvey common sense with a holy veneer. In his preaching, Rogers made great effort to exegete (read what is actually in the text, against its historical background) and exposit (explain and apply practically) the Bible for the benefit of all the congregation.

Rogers did not alter his style for special occasions. At funerals, for instance, he took the opportunity of pressing home Christian teaching by connecting biblical characters with the person who had died. At the funeral of Mrs Harvey, the widow of an army colonel, she was compared with the Jewess Eunice, mother of Timothy. Rogers took this opportunity to stress the important role played by Christian mothers in nurturing the faith of their children. While eyebrows may now be raised regarding what Rogers implied about gender roles — God has "Divinely appointed the Domestic Constitution for the highest and noblest purposes" — his valuing of motherhood is significant. He quoted from an 1838 letter from Mrs Harvey to her son in Ireland in which she delights to hear that his family continued to have morning and evening prayers together.

Another feature of St James' approach was belief in conversion. Rogers rejected the idea that people are "Christian" by virtue of culture, citizenship, parentage or even churchgoing. Indeed, to quote the Mrs Harvey funeral sermon[8] again, neither the Judaism of Eunice nor the privileges of being raised with "The Word of God as their guide — a pure worship, to warm the affections and improve the heart — appointed means of instruction, through a public ministry — festivals and sacraments . . ." were enough. Mere belief had to become "confidence . . . the imaginary becomes real; the object of all the promises becomes the subject of her dearest hopes; the promised Messiah is her Saviour."

If the need for conversion clearly was taught from earliest times at St James', it was also directly connected with the cross of Christ. Mrs Harvey's own testimony was that once "I was blind." But now, when "the eyes of the understanding had been opened," she could add, "but now I see!" Rogers affirmed this, but did not stop there. He asked "Is not the faith of too many, such in *name only*, proving its existence by no corresponding works . . .?"

Mrs Harvey's care for her children, and especially for their spiritual progress, was evidence to him of the reality of her faith. She also found that her "Religion wonderfully kept me up," particularly through trying separations from her children. At a time of great anxiety she confessed: "My great desire is to fulfil my duty, and do what I think is right, leaving the consequences to God." This again Rogers took as proof of the "great and radical change" made in her life by conversion to Christ. The stress on personal commitment shows that St James' stood for much more than mere anti-Catholicism.[9] Nonetheless, anti-Catholicism was important.

ST JAMES AGAINST "ROMANISM"

One of the great difficulties that churches like St James' perceived was the threat of Roman Catholicism. From the corner of Arch and Union Streets it seemed that the huge St Mary's church being built a few blocks away on Brock Street was the outpost of an evil empire. Local legend, probably based in fact, has it that while St Mary's was being built, a guard had to be posted to prevent Orange Order activists from removing the masonry under cover of darkness. Whether or not this is true, the Orange Lodges — fraternal societies commemorating the victory of William of Orange at the Battle of the Boyne in 1690 — did wield considerable influence in Kingston.

"In this part of the dominions and in our own immediate neighbourhood," warned Rogers, "look at the mighty preparations of Rome again to bring us into bondage . . ."[10] The challenge had to be met by "contending for the faith." Something so precious, bought at so great a price — "before whose eyes, Jesus Christ hath been evidently set forth, crucified" — was worth defending.

There was some hyperbole in the fear of an evil empire. The reason the Catholics were building was much the same as St James' own; the mid-century influx of Irish immigrants. Although Kingston Catholicism had been primarily Scottish — their best known leader, Alexander MacDonell, started as a "patriarchal and warlike"[11] chaplain to the Glengarry Fencibles — Irish arrivals brought

Roman Catholics to 32% of the Kingston population in 1851. But they came to a city already notorious for its politically Protestant presence. One reason why Kingston lost its grip on capital status was that, in Robert Baldwin's words, it was an "Orange hole."[12] Even John A. Macdonald, despite his conciliatory attitude to Catholics, was an Orangeman.[13]

Probably the most notorious Orange-led fiasco in Kingston happened in 1860 when the young Prince of Wales was scheduled to visit the city after opening the new iron girder bridge in Montreal and laying the parliament building cornerstone in Ottawa. St James' member William Shannon was chairman of the Orange Order Reception Committee[14] and Anthony O'Loughlin, churchwarden, was commissioned to make and carve a chair for his highness.[15]

Controversy between the Orange Order and Catholics erupted over the nature of and budget for the reception. The prince's uncle, Duke Henry of Newcastle, was adamant that there be no "partisan displays." So when the Orangemen erected arches over Princess Street and 15,000 banner-waving supporters showed up in full regalia (from 54 area lodges) he was not impressed. The steamer *City of Kingston* only got close enough for the prince to hear 500 children singing to him from another steamer, *Hercules*, before moving on to Belleville for what turned out to be a repeat performance![16] The beautifully carved chair was never used.[17]

Anthony O'Loughlin's chair, crafted for the Prince of Wales visit to Kingston, 1860.

The Orangemen Arch, Princess Street, 1860 (QUA).

St James' Orange Lodge members were undoubtedly among the crowd that inadvertently prevented the royal visit. But as far as St James' was concerned the case against Rome was that its gospel deviated in essentials from the simplicity of faith in Christ crucified. Additions were made, in the shape of images, rituals, priestly power and so on, that deflected attention from Jesus as the way to God. Thus "popery" could be seen as a "masterpiece of Satan," in which the "dark system of Heathenism is covered over with the brightness of Christianity." Evidence of malevolent intent was found in the annually re-published papal Bull that "excommunicated and accused" all "Hussites, Wickliffites, Lutherans . . . Anabaptists, Trinitarians and apostates from the Christian faith . . ." among whom Protestant Anglicans would number themselves. Beyond this was a fear that political freedom was also jeopardized by the spread of Romanism, "that great confederacy against civil liberties . . ."

Despite the impassioned tone of Rogers' repudiation of Rome, he was at pains to distance himself from any forms of direct action. When asked by some in the congregation who were members of the Loyal Orange Lodge Society — James Shannon was Grand Secretary for Central Canada[18] — to address them on the anniversary of the landing of William of Orange, he urged their "prayerful consideration" for the thought that the good of Catholics, not victory over them, should be sought. We could surmise that Anthony O'Loughlin also took a conciliatory approach. He was a great supporter of Catholic-agitator-turned-Canadian-nationalist D'Arcy McGee (and also, it is said, shared the soft Irish brogue of his oratorical style).

It is Roman*ism*, not Roman*ists* that deserve censure, argued Rogers. Would it be inflammatory to teach our children the simple way of Christ? Would it "kindle party strife? God forbid!" was his feisty riposte. The "spirit of Christ" would suggest a better way: "This ought to be the desire of every Protestant in his intercourse with Romanists 'by pureness, by knowledge, by longsuffering, by kindness, by the Holy Ghost, by *love* unfeigned, (2 Cor. vi.6) to convince the gainsayers.'"[19]

THE ENEMY WITHIN: CREEPING CATHOLICISM

In fact, St James' seems to have been more concerned about resisting the spread of Roman Catholicism *within* the church than attacking it outside. While Rogers certainly likened Catholic*ism* to Babylon or the pope to the anti-Christ of the book of Revelation, he was conciliatory towards actual Catholic friends and neighbours in the streets and homes of Stuartville. His attitude towards those who, he thought, would defile the church for which he worked with the destructive doctrines of Rome was far more fierce and fiery.

In nineteenth century Canada relations between Catholics and Protestants were strained, to say the least. Within the Church of England, the Oxford Movement — or Tractarians — caused a split between high church (ritualistic, Catholic-oriented) and two other groups, often lumped together as "low church." In fact, all that low church and evangelicals had in common was their opposition to Rome. Low church people were often deist and doubted just what the evangelicals affirmed — biblical inspiration, vicarious atonement and the deity of Christ.[20]

Kingston was generally opposed to Rome, and St James' was a prominent example. Thus any moves within the church that seemed to signal Romeward shifts were regarded with suspicion and as the occasion for rebuke. Those so criticised could give as good as they got, and the low church factions and evangelical groups received everything from haughty denials to counter-accusation.

As early as 1846 St James' objected to the dedication of the new church building on Queen Street to "Saint Paul." What was the problem? Church buildings could be *distinguished* by biblical names, but *dedicated* only to God's glory. The controversy broke out at a meeting of the Church Society, after which George Okill Stuart stepped in to try to conciliate. A further meeting took place at St George's, when the Church Society secretary tried to reassure all present that no special significance was attached to the phrase "dedicated to St Paul."

The Church had no problem with this and believed the objectors to be "straining at gnats." But *The Berean*, which took the evangelical side, urged that much more was at stake. If the Reformation had got rid of "erroneous and strange doctrines" of saints, then the "enlightened Anglican" should resist their restoration "in its incipient stage of seed-sowing." Such have to "watch for souls." The pastor knows such souls "cannot be saved by service to Saints, Martyrs, or Angels: not to these therefore does he dedicate the places of worship which he has helped building, but to God who gave his Son, and to the Saviour who was crucified for sinners."[21]

Twenty years later, in 1867, the same fears were still being expressed, only on this occasion they were sparked by a sung service in a schoolroom on Division Street (later to become a St George's chapel of ease). St James' viewed this "with alarm" because in England such sung services had, according to them, "preceded the adoption of a more expressive ritual." The bishop responded quickly, saying that it "would not have occurred to anyone who knew its history" to connect sung services with Rome, as they had been encouraged by none other than Archbishop Cranmer, the prayer book compiler, to "encite the hearts of all men to devotion to godliness."[22]

The bishop then turned on St James' with the words "It would tend to greater practical activity if instead of throwing unfounded aspersions on the service in Division Street, you would turn your attention to the flagrant breaches of the Rubrics which occur in St James' Church, with a view to their correction."[23] This was an unexpected charge, and one to which the St James' vestry could only reply that they "knew nothing" of such breaches. As for Cranmer, they said, the reason he had accepted sung services was simple; he had yet to realize the full implications of his Protestant faith when he did so! In short, St James' people concluded that they had to "differ with our bishop altogether and arrive at a directly opposite conclusion to his . . ."

Other examples may be given of the vigorously Protestant character of St James', from the collection for "converts from Popery in Ireland"[24] to the congregational disapproval of doctrines being taught at Trinity College, Toronto. Many years later, similar themes still appear in the minute books, including objections to those who wished to add articles of "Romish" furniture such as "credence" shelves, in memory of parishioners who would heartily have repudiated their use! Whatever we make of this today it is clear that the men and women comprising the early vestry meetings at St James' knew clearly what they believed and were keen to preserve and defend it.[25]

CLERICAL OR LAY LEADERS?

One important effect of the Catholic-Protestant controversies was to encourage so-called lay leadership in the church. In all the situations mentioned above, it was members of vestry that took the initiative. The rector clearly gave a lead, but was not regarded as being above criticism or of leading single-handedly. The names of Arthur O'Loughlin, William Shannon, Thomas Agnew (perhaps of Agnew's Lane, renamed William Street 1885), E.R. Welch, Edward Pense keep reappearing in the lists of those committed to one resolution or another.

One of these, Arthur O'Loughlin, argued in a Church Society meeting in 1862 that clergy should "specially invite the intelligent, active and zealous cooperation of the laity as necessary to the welfare of this Society and that of our beloved church."[26] He pursued a dogged path of just such zeal, serving in the church and beyond. He continued the tradition, started by Rogers, of work in the penitentiary, although by this time he had begun studies that would take him from cabinet-making to join the ranks of the clergy in 1863. William Shannon, likewise, found himself filling almost every lay position in the church over a period of more than a decade, from selling concert tickets to being a Synod delegate. As someone observed, "the nature of the numerous resolutions he sponsored showed that he was not a placid, passive, pliable church officer who stood in awe of the cloth."[27]

When eventually Rogers resigned the rectorship in 1869, yet another dispute arose, this time over his successor. Not surprisingly, the vestry dearly wanted his assistant, W.B. Moffett, to take over, but the bishop had other ideas. When Moffett was refused on the grounds, among others, that "there were other and older clergymen in the diocese who had greater claim to the place," the vestry suggested two further names — Dobbs and Henderson — for consideration. When in the end the bishop won the day this was bad news for his appointee, Francis Kirkpatrick, who had to take office knowing that he was far from the first choice of rector. How he emerged from under that cloud is told later. The bid for stronger lay leadership was very significant, but it failed in this case. Clearly, this time the bishop called the shots.[28]

Such lay leadership was stimulated by more than one factor. It is certainly the case that solely clerical leadership was distrusted as Romish. All believers, the Reformers had taught, are equal before God, and this is seen both in their being equally justified by faith alone and in their having equal duties to spread the good news of God's love and rule. Evangelicals in early Canadian synods fought — and failed — to have this equality extended to voting rights.[29] At St James', lay leaders were prominent, even though rectors also had their own agendas. Before too long, women too would become pastoral lay leaders, although it would be a long time before their contribution was fully recognised.

The other contributory factor behind lay leadership at St James' was its relative financial independence. St James' was a "free" church which not only meant that the Archdeacon had no direct control over it, but that it also had to find its own funding. When in 1854 the Clergy Reserves had been taken over by the state after long wrangles, alternatives had to be found to replace these income-generating land endowments. Ordinary parishioners had to dig into their pockets to provide for the church and in turn came to expect more participation in decision-making. For some clergy this appeared as an alien "democracy" movement, but at St James' little evidence of direct lay-clergy conflict exists at this time.

FORGING AN EVANGELICAL IDENTITY

By the end of the nineteenth century the dominant religious spirit in Ontario Protestantism was evangelical. St James' was as much associated with evangelicalism as it was with Anglicanism. So what is meant by "evangelicalism?" Four elements are central: the Bible, the cross, conversion and activism.[30] We have seen in this chapter how the first three certainly were important to St James'. In the next, activism is central, and completes the picture of St James' as a congregation with an evangelical emphasis.

We have also noted the role played, for better and for worse, by anti-Catholicism in the development of an evangelical ethos. Resurgent Rome, plus the influx of Irish immigrants, made it unsurprising that anti-Catholicism should surface in Kingston and especially at St James'. Anti-Catholicism connects with the four features of evangelicalism. "Popery" tended to obscure the relevance of a clear (though perhaps gradual) conversion and kept people away from a direct appreciation of Scripture. It also seemed to add other items to the cross as the sole means of salvation. Lastly, it catalysed Protestant activism, especially in the drive to outdo the best efforts of Rome.[31]

Rogers, for instance, was on the committee of the Kingston Auxiliary Bible Society (related to the BFBS) in 1855, along with leaders from other (Methodist and Presbyterian) churches. The KABS existed to promote access to and readership of the Bible which "alone — pure, undiminished and without addition is our shield — our lamp — our chart. The bulwark of liberty, civil and religious, the safeguard of domestic virtue and peace."[32] But it also stood against Catholicism which, they said, inhibited popular Bible use, and amounted to religious bondage. As it happens, the KABS also helped to show the extent of material poverty, as its agents went from home to home. Rogers, as someone committed to the ordinary people, often poor, in Stuartville, would also have approved this aspect of the work.

It would be a mistake to imagine, however, that the only challenge came from Rome. St James' also responded to apparent attacks from other quarters. In 1860, for example, only a year after the publication of Charles Darwin's *the Origin of Species*, layperson O'Loughlin could be heard holding forth against the evils of this "atheistic" doctrine in a special lecture held at City Hall. His talk, "Man, a Material, Mental and Spiritual being," attracted a crowd from varied backgrounds, including clergy from different denominations, professors from Queen's College and "persons professional and otherwise distinguished for their literary attainments."[33] St James' people were active on a number of fronts, "defending the faith" from moral,

intellectual and social threats.

Without doubt, St James' saw itself as an evangelical church. When asking for a say in who should be bishop, St James' vestry stressed the need for a "moderate" and "evangelical." When stating the purposes of the Church Society, they observed that it should be "Protestant and Evangelical." They would have concurred with the English cleric, J.C. Ryle, writing in the *Evangelical Churchman*, that "The times we live in are desperately unfavourable to a sharply-cut, decided, distinct, doctrinal Christianity."[34] Such views remained strong in Ontario until well after the turn of the century.

Claiming that the "day of polemics . . . and dogmatism" is gone, Dyson Hague — one-time rector of Brockville who preached periodically at St James' — had this to say of evangelicalism:

For as long as a man is a sinner and stands guilty before a Holy God, the Gospel that tells him he can be justified by faith only through Christ's work for him, and Christ's work in him, and as long as that is preached by loving, sympathetic and earnest men, so long in Canada or anywhere else, will it have its future.[35] That, in a nutshell, was how nineteenth (and for that matter twentieth) century evangelicals understood the gospel.

Subsequent chapters will show how St James' managed to hold onto that "sharply cut" Christianity *and* simultaneously to mellow its views of the papist threat. By the turn of the century the building would contain a chancel, communion would be more frequent, and a robed choir would soon lead the worship. But reformational principles continued to count for a lot, even after some signs of tractarianism had been quietly accepted. Some Rome-watchers would not relax their vigilance, however, until the later twentieth century.

By the later nineteenth century, evangelicalism was the predominant religious and cultural force in Ontario.[36] Through the evangelical press and contacts with other like-minded congregations in Toronto, Montreal and elsewhere, a network was emerging.[37] This and her strong contacts with other local — but not necessarily Anglican — churches gave St James' Church an identity within Kingston that was as much related to a growing indigenous Canadian evangelicalism as it was to its mother, the United Church of England and Ireland.

3

A Social Conscience

*"Be not drunk with wine, wherein is excess;
but be filled with the Spirit. . ."*

— Ephesians 5:17

In 1857 there were about 162 licensed drinking taverns in Kingston, plus many unlicensed "dives" and "blind pigs."[1] This in a city of only about 12,000! The military presence was largely blamed for this state of affairs, although the influx of Irish people was also thought to be a contributing factor. Back in 1840 the Kingston *Chronicle* had complained that "Disguise it as we may, the streets of Kingston are night and day swarming with drunkards and prostitutes, and never since we have been residents of the town have we seen so much vice as now prevails, and which seems to be daily increasing."[2] The demon drink would continue to exercise public attention well into the twentieth century.

In response to this situation several Kingston branches of the Independent Order of Good Templars were established, along with other Temperance Societies. St James', with the drill hall just across Arch Street, and taverns on nearby Wellington Street was sharply aware of the problem, and its own branch of the Church of England Temperance Society was set up in 1875, and flourished until the turn of the century.

So while nearby taverns echoed to the sounds of raucous drinking songs, down the road at St James' different music could be heard, no doubt including this gem:

> Lord of heav'n and earth! assist us,
> While the temperance cause we plead,
> Though both earth and hell resist us,
> If Thou bless, we must succeed;
> > From intemperance
> > May our country soon be freed.[3]

We do not know what tune was used, but Cwm Rhondda fits, appropriately.

In this chapter, the story of St James' is seen largely in terms of its social conscience and its activism. Chronologically, it takes us beyond the work of Robert Rogers and into the decade and a half of Francis Kirkpatrick's ministry (1869–1885), whose biography appears at the end of the chapter. Both leaders were tireless activists, but it was Kirkpatrick who focussed his zeal in the temperance cause. Both leaders inherited views of disadvantaged people that might today be considered paternalistic, but this in no way implies that their concern was less than genuine and heartfelt. Better this than complacency! However, it may mean that they did not always perceive the root causes of social disadvantage.

On the one hand, St James' can be seen as a microcosm of Canadian history. The number of ordinary lay people involved in public life out of Christian conviction peaked in these years.[4] Temperance was one of several causes into which enthusiastic Christian citizens threw themselves as a way of trying to cope with the growing pressures of urban, industrial society.[5] On the other, when temperance was more usually associated with Methodism, St James', even though it had its own brewing connections, was distinctive as an Anglican church that retained strong ties with other churches in the city.

Victorian Ontario cannot be understood without a consideration of temperance movements. They were linked with hope for a better, more moral future, interpreted as signs of God's coming kingdom.[6] They gave first-time opportunities for women to be socially, and sometimes politically, involved. And the St James' case is classic as a crucible for working out how personal salvation and social reform were connected. As we shall see, the temperance movement was just the most prominent way in which St James' expressed its social conscience.

ST JAMES' AND THE GROWTH OF KINGSTON

When St James' was founded, the future of Kingston as a major Canadian town seemed clear. Much of the history of Canada was being made in its streets and buildings. Huge hope — and speculative investment — lay in the choice of Kingston as the capital city. When after three short years that honour was relocated to Montreal, the redundant buildings and a sense of something owing to Kingston, remained. During St James' first 50 years, Kingston was steadily ousted from the position it had held in 1830 as Upper Canada's premier town. Toronto (and even Hamilton) had overtaken Kingston in size by 1851, and by the turn of the century (1901) had left Kingston far behind; 208,040 to Kingston's mere 17,961.

Nonetheless, Kingston contributed considerably to the political and cultural life of Canada, and also adopted similar transport and technology innovations to other, larger cities. Sir John A. Macdonald attended at the

Confederation ceremony in Market Square, 1867, and he also opened the dry dock in 1890. Gas lighting illuminated the streets from 1847, horse-drawn street cars began operating in 1877, and went electric in 1893, just five years after electricity was introduced in Kingston. The Kingston and Pembroke — "Kick and Push" — Railway began in 1871, the telephone system started ten years later, although the first water works were not established until 1887. St James' people were involved, in roles ranging from the labourers who built and ran these systems to the businessmen who owned them.

Although material and social stability increased in the Stuartville of the 1860s and 1870s, the problems of poverty and alcohol abuse did not disappear overnight. While St James' attempted to address these through its support for the Widows and Orphans Fund and the Poor Fund, it also promoted sobriety through the St James' Temperance Society.

ST JAMES' FOR THE POOR

None of the social welfare agencies we know today existed in mid-nineteenth century Kingston. Yet social problems, some of a dire and chronic nature, were widespread. Stuartville was one area where these problems were often manifest in a particularly acute form. While nothing matched the intensity of suffering that came with the cholera epidemic of 1847, the ongoing hardships of new immigrants seeking employment

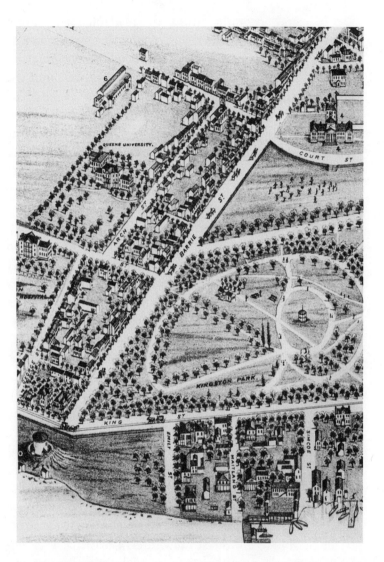

Brosius map of 1875 shows St James' and the shed mentioned by contemporary observers. St James' parishioners lived in the Barrie, Union, Arch and Division Street houses. Note the horse-drawn street car on King Street (QUA).

and accommodation, the inadequacy of poorer housing for the rigors of a harsh Ontario winter, and the health risks of a newly-urban area still presented a considerable challenge well after the mid-century period.

It was commonly assumed that churches, along with extended families, were the first line of response to such social crises. Other agencies existed, such as the Kingston Compassionate Society, the Orphan Home and Widow's Friend Society and the Midland District School Society, and churches were often associated with these. It is true that from 1847 a House of Industry had been available, supported in part by a small city tax from 1849. This was made compulsory by the Municipal Institutions Act of 1866. But the House of Industry ran a pretty harsh regime, aimed at helping only the so-called deserving poor. The Irish, most populous in Stuartville, were the main users of the House of Industry.[7]

St James' was as least as deeply involved in attempting to alleviate social problems as any other church. Probably, given its location, more so. A system of parish visitation by women was in place for many years. It had particular concern for widows and those made vulnerable by other loss of income. The system also tried to ensure that sufficient fuel and warm clothing were available to all to last the winter. Christmas was regularly preceded by a special collection for the poor of the parish.

The extent of poverty was hard to gauge, but would have been obvious to the members of the St James' congregation, both through their dealings with the Midland District School, which was primarily for poorer children, and the jail, and through other agencies. For instance, the Bible Society conducted door-to-door visiting that had the side-effect of revealing just how deprived were the conditions behind the front doors of some Stuartville residents. Certainly in the early days of St James' poverty was considerable. Poor drainage and sanitation created health hazards which gave Stuartville triple the mortality rate of the rest of Kingston and many people were crowded into rented accommodation.[8]

Poor relief was one of several activities in which women were prominent, no doubt reflecting the dual role that women played as daytime neighbours as well as church members. Women were involved in the visiting work, and in the distribution of clothing and food to the poor. When Alice Rogers (Robert Rogers' daughter-in-law) died in 1899 it was her "philanthropy" and her concern "for the suffering of all classes, regardless of creed" that were singled out for notice.

In the days before any organised health system, searches were constantly made for cures for all kinds of ailments, and these were routinely reported in the press. Robert Rogers, for instance, who had lost a daughter to scarlet fever in 1848, offered to the public details of a "water cure" that had apparently worked when his five year old son had the same symptoms.

Stating his intent to "relieve suffering humanity, if not save life" he wrote to the *Kingston Chronicle and News*, describing the way he had wrapped the boy in a wet sheet covered with blankets around 8.00 a.m., following the first "premonitory symptoms" at 5.00 a.m. The only medicine given was "a teaspoonful of castor oil and an injection of spirits of turpentine." A few days later when his seven year old son and infant daughter fell victims to the fever, the same treatment was tried, to good effect. Rogers expressed his "heartfelt gratitude to God for his blessing on the means" of restoring his children to health, and a Dr Mair, Assistant Staff Surgeon, declared himself "highly satisfied with the results."[9]

Concern for ordinary people, and especially for the more disadvantaged, continued after Rogers retired. Kirkpatrick saw to it, for instance, that seating was free on Sunday evenings so that — patronizing as it may sound — the poorest were not excluded. Further afield, the church also supported the "Irish Relief" programme in 1880. Within a few years, full-scale relief and aid work was under way, to help poorer dioceses such as Algoma and to raise the standard of living of native peoples in touch with Anglican missions there and beyond.

ST JAMES' TEMPERANCE SOCIETY

The St James' Temperance Society was founded on Ash Wednesday, February 13 1875. It existed to ". . . protest against a vice which has done and is doing so much to injure society, and to which the ruin of so many persons can be distinctly traced." Although part of a broader social reform movement, the Society placed its greatest hope in the "Divine agency of the gospel." Why? Because intemperance was a sin, so "while the cure of the vice may be attained by a plan of total abstinence, the pardon of the *sin* can only be had 'through the blood of Jesus Christ our Lord.'"[10]

Part of the initiative lay in the Church of England Temperance Society, which is also where the open membership policy originated. One could be either a total abstainer or a moderate drinker. A member agreed to a first "Christian duty" to "exert myself for the suppression of intemperance." Beyond this, members would "in the name of the Lord Jesus Christ" promote the objects of the Society or "with the help of God, . . . abstain from the use of all intoxicating drinks."[11] Perhaps the drinkers (and brewers?) in the congregation had left or changed their views by 1878 because in February that year a motion was made to change the name to the "St James' Total Abstinence Society."

Membership was open also to women and

men, who served alongside each other on the committee. Alice Rogers and a Miss Wilson helped lead the meetings for a number of years. Miss Fanny Dupuy, the church organist, played for the temperance meetings. Less successful, it seems, were the attempts to involve young people in the junior section, the "Band of Hope." In other places they too would sing temperance songs, take "the pledge" and engage in consciousness raising events about the evil effects of alcohol abuse, but the St James' chapter lasted only a short time.[12]

Regular meetings were held on the second Tuesday of each month, except for a break in the summer, but special meetings were also held, for which a more general invitation was issued. Ordinary meetings would include hymn and song-singing and prayer. But there would also be musical items or dramatic performances, especially so in the case of special meetings. In April 1890, Robert Rogers (the first rector's son), a lawyer, gave a spirited rendition of the chariot race in *Ben Hur*. In February 1891 Miss Corbett recited a story of a poor London waif — "the story was pathetic," says the report, "startling in the novelty of its conception and excellently rendered." Discussions of issues like government regulation of liquor traffic, military temperance work or the effects of alcohol on the human body also took place. Principal George Grant of Queen's — not an abstainer! — came more than once as a visiting speaker.

Major Edwards of the Royal Military College made some lively contributions to St James' Temperance Society meetings in 1890 and 1891. For him, moderation was a "higher virtue" than abstinence: "As, however, there are many weak natures by whom such self control is almost unattainable he insisted upon Total Abstinence as in their case an absolute necessity, and the abstainers he described as the vanguard, the backbone, the soul and forlorn hope of the Temperance army, without whose help the fortress of intemperance would never be stormed successfully . . . "
Obviously a committed anglophone, at one Temperance meeting Edwards "denounced the obnoxious custom of encoring, as involving the use of an unEnglish word, unduly prolonging the programme and making invidious distinctions. In spite of all, the major's alternative suggestion was accepted and he was rapturously recalled with shouts of 'now again.'"[13]

On a practical level, the St James' Society offered help to those, including parishioners, struggling with alcohol-related issues. "Even in our own congregation," it was reported in 1880, "the evil claims its victims." Some, it was said, "have from time to time fallen back under the pressure of temptation and yielded themselves to the evil which, in their better moments, they so freely recognise.'[14] Committee members of the Kingston

Temperance Society, which no doubt operated like the St James' Society, had the responsibility of speaking privately to those seen "violating the pledge," to reprove them in "a friendly manner," and, if they failed to mend their ways, to erase their names from the list of members.[15]

From the start, Francis Kirkpatrick emphasized the spiritual aspect of the struggle with the power of strong drink; no merely secular temperance movement would be equal to it. If "too little prominence" was given to the "duties of repentance and faith" then temperance movements would fail, he insisted. If the first article of the temperance creed did not confess that "the Gospel of Christ is the only care for the blight of sin which is so widespread" then it had no place in the church.[16] Restricting the sale of liquor and encouraging self-restraint had its role, but no *lasting* cure for intemperance could be found "outside the Church."

St James' Temperance Society clearly made its mark in the city. In January 1881 *The British Whig* reported a visit from the secretary of the Church of England Temperance Society, Robert Graham, who noted that the only "live" temperance groups in Kingston were at St James' and at the "B" battery. "From his limited experience he judged that the drunkenness in this country is not half what it is in the old country. In Canada he had not seen the poverty which he had witnessed at home. This colony has a great future before it, but the people must see that the liquor traffic does not get a hold of its vitals."[17]

And this is the man with keg and jar,
That stands behind his tavern bar,
And swears how good his liquors are,
And slyly keeps his door ajar—
Enticing the drunkard tattered and torn,
Whose wife and children weep forlorn,
And share this world's cold, cruel scorn.

The temperance villain was the bartender shown here in a Toronto-published book, *The Flood of Death* by Archibald McKillip (1875).

And this is the man at holy shrine,
Who loves the clusters of the vine,
And says that God with kind design
Has made intoxicating wine,
And even whiskey—a boon divine.
Who teaches the Christian saved from sin,
Who hopes eternal life to win,—
Yet stands aside with tearless eye,
And sees his fellow-creatures die.

Anglicans were not normally associated with the temperance movement!

Although the main leader for many years was Kirkpatrick, concern about alcohol abuse was nothing new. Robert Rogers had been elected vice-president of the Kingston branch of the Canadian Temperance League back in 1853. At that time, the aim was to advocate a "prohibition liquor law."[18] After Kirkpatrick died in 1885, the new rector, John McMorine, carried the temperance torch at St James' until the Society was disbanded in 1900, and then within the newly formed Diocesan Church Temperance Society, for which he was a committee member until his retirement in 1909.

The Dunkin Act of 1864 gave authority to municipalities in Canada East and Canada West to prohibit liquor, but Kingston voted to stay wet. The Church of England Temperance Society, of which St James' was a branch, wished at least to encourage the upholding of law, but focussed mainly on promoting temperance habits, helping alcohol abusers and removing the causes of intemperance. At a diocesan level this work was continued, but on a more general basis, in the early twentieth century. From 1910 temperance work was subsumed under the Committee on Moral and Social Reform which among other things tried to enforce an eleven p.m. closing time for pool rooms which were evidently "becoming a serious menace to public morals in cities and university towns."[19] Rector Thomas Savery was a member of that committee.

EVANGELICALS AND THE SOCIAL GOSPEL

Although some important impetus for the turn-of-the-century "Social Gospel" came from evangelicals, St James' would likely have been at the conservative end of the spectrum.[20] No evidence from the Temperance Society suggests that this church was committed to a social gospel as such. Not that their gospel had no social dimensions; indeed, these were crucially important. But at least from Kirkpatrick the message was plain, the gospel must never be *reduced* to the social.

St James' gospel brought hope in Christ to any sinners, among whom the inebriate might be numbered. The demands of the gospel included trying to remove what were seen to be the causes of intemperance, whether the late night pool rooms or the lax liquor laws. Like many other Ontario evangelicals, St James' people would have placed themselves in the tradition of the English "Clapham Sect" and of Lord Shaftesbury who, first following the revivals of the eighteenth century "were in the forefront of the great battle for the betterment of social, industrial, hygienic and economic conditions for the working classes."[21]

The fact that Queen's Principal George Grant was a visitor to the St James' Temperance Society must have had some impact. As economic depression came to an end in the early 1890s few were as active as Grant in catalysing Christian discussion of economic problems, poverty, socialism and social evolution. He founded the Queen's Theological Alumni Conference for this purpose in 1893, at which the Methodist social gospeller, Salem Bland, was probably the most radical participant.[22] Grant himself shared with some St James' people some paternalistic attitudes. His came from Presbyterian echoes of Knox's Scotland; St James' from the sense of social duty attached to being part of a once established church.

Within the diocese, more general social concerns than just temperance were expressed in the Committee on Moral and Social Reform from 1910. They claimed some success in the reduction of liquor licenses in the city from 25 to 15, but were also interested in the question of juvenile crime and Sunday Observance.[23] Removing "the social and moral conditions that make the cross of Christ of none effect" was how Bishop Edward John Bidwell described the objects of the committee. By 1917 this was renamed the Social Service Committee,[24] extending its scope again to immigration and the war effort.

That St James' possessed a social conscience is clear. Exactly how that was expressed, and with what effects, is a little more ambiguous. A lingering paternalism, and steadily increasing relative affluence, perhaps prevented St James' from seriously coming to grips with the realities of social disadvantage in Kingston. Moreover, it has been suggested that temperance movements, by concentrating on the demon drink, could deflect attention from the underlying social malaise of poverty.

While St James' people such as Kirkpatrick gave sterling service to the community, and through poor relief and temperance St James' showed concern for body-and-soul, one wonders if more could not have been done to express the social dimensions of the gospel. The crusading spirit of anti-slavery and prison reform once exhibited by Rogers was being dulled into energetic but respectable philanthropy by the turn of the century.

PROFILE
FRANCIS KIRKPATRICK
RECTOR 1869-1885

Francis Kirkpatrick was born October 5 1839, son of Thomas Kirkpatrick, a lawyer, and the first mayor of Kingston. He attended Kingston Grammar School before sailing for Ireland, where he studied for his BA and MA at Trinity College, Dublin. He completed his divinity course in 1861, walking off with the "Dr Downes's Divinity Premium" prize. He was ordained deacon in St George's Belfast, and was curate of Cumber in Ireland for two years.

Kirkpatrick returned to Canada West in 1864 to take charge of the Mission to Wolfe Island. Five years later, to the great disappointment of Wolfe Islanders, the bishop asked him to move back into Kingston, and to St James'. The congregation, already in some turmoil after the resignation of Robert Rogers, was doubly disturbed when their request was denied to have the curate, W.B. Moffett, take over. Understandably, Kirkpatrick received a somewhat cool reception.

The thirty-year-old Kirkpatrick was equal to this challenge, however, and made it his priority steadily to gain the confidence of the congregation through sheer hard work and devoted commitment. Perhaps to the surprise of the church he turned out to have similar traits to Rogers: "Though decided and outspoken on doctrinal points," it was said, he "drew men to him by the gentler ways and out of the preaching of a pure gospel."[25] At the church jubilee in 1895 Kirkpatrick would be remembered like this; "He had not the eloquence of Paul, but he had the zeal of Peter and the love of John."[26]

To compare Francis Kirkpatrick with his much better known brother — George Airey Kirkpatrick, president of the Canadian Locomotive and Engine Company, Kingston MP, Speaker of the House of Commons and Lieutenant Governor — is a study in contrasts. Where George was flamboyant, aristocratic and a man of "large private means,"[27] Francis was just the opposite. Described as "the Good Samaritan," he made daily rounds not only in the parish but beyond, visiting the poor, the sick and the grieving. On occasion he would dig into his own pocket to help "the needy." He was, said a clergy colleague, ". . . habitually indifferent to all personal comforts, and indeed, to a fault regardless of those indulgences which, for others' sake, he persistently denied himself."[28]

Kirkpatrick's wife, Emily Gertrude, seems to have worked alongside him as the unpaid helper. Little is known about her, though she was later involved in the Woman's Auxiliary. She outlived him by twenty-three years, dying in 1908. Their son, Francis, also became an Anglican minister, and members of the Kirkpatrick family worship at St James' to this day.

As a minister he clearly saw himself as an encourager, an enabler of others. He tried to persuade the congregation that it is a "sacred duty to swell the voice of prayer and praise. Hearty responses add much to the enjoyment of public worship. . . ."[29] He urged them to come out to the Wednesday evening Bible study meeting. And he recommended that they take proper holidays from work, advice he seemed unable to follow himself: "Crowded into our towns and cities, our mills and offices and shops, we are so oppressively surrounded by the works of man. Man built the houses, paved the streets and strung the telegraph wires and fashioned the engines . . . It is our best refreshment to get away, where only God's working seems to be around us."[30] (It is interesting to note, in passing, that telegraph wires were strung in Kingston from 1848; Kirkpatrick wrote this in 1879, the year the first telephone was installed in Kingston at Rockwood Asylum.)

Kirkpatrick was also deeply involved in numerous organizations in Kingston and beyond. Within the Anglican Church he was rural dean of Frontenac, having responsibility for the oversight of a number of churches, and was especially active on the missions committees of the Ontario Synod. His mission interest also took him to the diocese of Algoma (near Arthur's Landing, now Sudbury, Ontario) where he worked as bishop's commissary, building up the work in native schools. As president of the Bible Society and actively involved in the Religious

Francis Kirkpatrick probably in the mid-1870s.

Francis Kirkpatrick's portrait shows his temperance medal (c. 1880).

Tract Society, Sabbath Reformation Society and the Evangelical Alliance, he worked alongside many other Kingstonians from different churches, winning their affection and admiration.

The work for which he is best remembered, however, is the Temperance Movement, and the St James' branch of the Temperance Society. He was eventually awarded a medal by the Society in April 1878 which can be seen in his portrait in the Rogers' Room at St James'. This was the aspect of his work into which he put more energy than any other.

In the middle of all this apparently indefatigable activity, his death in 1885 at age 45 came as a huge shock, not only to St James' but to Kingston. The congregation, concerned about his evident weariness, persuaded his to visit Algoma in the later summer, and he bounced back energetically. He planned a mission during the fall, which he ran with a fellow minister, F. H. Du Vernet, before Christmas. On Christmas Eve he agreed to take the funeral of a parishioner from Wolfe Island days. This involved a frigid steamer trip to the point at which the ice had already formed, a walk to shore, and a sleigh-ride for several hours. He caught a cold,

fainted during Christmas communion the next day, and died a few days afterwards of "typhoid-pneumonia."

So New Year 1886 was anything but happy in Stuartville. The funeral was very well attended, with the nave and gallery filled to overcapacity and hundreds more outside in Union Street. They sang "Jesus I am resting, resting" and several others of his favourite hymns. There was no address at the funeral, at his request, but sermons throughout the city on the following Sunday were stretched to include grateful and generous references to him. As it coincided with the five hundredth anniversary of the death of Wycliffe, some even made comments connecting Kirkpatrick's concerns with the reformer's.[31] Despite the difficult beginning to his ministry, it was said that he left the church "in great harmony, as one happy family."[32]

The long slow march all the way to Cataraqui Cemetery included both the prominent citizens of the city, there to pay their respects, and many of the "poor and thinly clad," shivering against a grey, cold day. The comment of many of the latter spoke volumes about the man: "We shall miss him this winter."[33]

4

Growing Neighbourhood

"We had five churches: the Anglican, poor but believed to have some mysterious social supremacy; the Presbyterian, solvent and thought — chiefly by itself — to be intellectual; the Methodist, insolvent and fervent; the Baptist, insolvent and saved; the Roman Catholic, mysterious to most of us but clearly solvent. . . "

— Robertson Davies[1]

A special church meeting held on September 26 1887 produced a decision to let the building be "abandoned to the mason." Construction was to start again, with the side walls being removed and the building widened (double transept) and lengthened (a chancel). The number of people wishing to attend St James' had grown, and it was time to find more accommodation for them. The aim was to double the number of seats. If the available statistics are reliable, by 1894 the total population of St James' had climbed to 975. If the sanctuary was full, then perhaps up to 500 would attend on a Sunday (see Appendix I).

It had not been an easy decision, however. Earlier in 1887, the Easter vestry meeting had turned down the rebuilding plan on the grounds that no tenders could be found under $10,000. After a flurry of searching, however, a new tender came in at $8,500. This one was to succeed. Edward Pense, churchwarden, chaired the September meeting and observed that church finances were in very good shape; almost no debt! Joseph Power, the architect, showed various plans for extension, none of which exceeded the budget. It was noted that "A number of ladies were present, and took a warm interest in the proceedings," and that the eventual vote for the plans was near unanimous.[2]

By March 1888, due to the enthusiastic work of the men and women on the canvassing committee, nearly $3000 had been pledged and work was about to commence. So that winter the church met in the small western wing room on the second floor of the Court House, reached through the Barrie Street door. Meanwhile the building was buttressed and scaffolded, walls were removed and new stone brought from the quarry to construct the new chancel and the two side sections. Despite a resolution from the building committee[3] expressing dissatisfaction with the failure of some trades to complete on time and a reluctant decision to drop plans for frescoes and decorative plaster work because of rising costs, the work was finally complete. This was when the building took the shape by which it is known today.

Thus the nave was widened by twelve-and-a-half feet transepts on each side, a chancel was made with an organ chamber and three gothic porches. The chancel, with its stained glass, was a memorial to the first two rectors. (The third, John Kerr McMorine, was rector at the time of these alterations, having started his ministry in 1885. His life story is told at the end of this chapter.)

Two hot air furnaces were also installed. These replaced the two wood stoves, one on each side of the entrance which had warmed the building by means of stove pipes running the whole length of the nave. Over time, the pipes had rusted as water had entered them from above, so that in bad weather pails were placed

| The newly extended building, 1888.

under the pipe gutters to collect the leaking sooty water.[4]

The expansion of the building reflected a growing need for more space for the church, which in turn indicated a growing neighbourhood — in a slowly but steadily growing city — and continuing good prospects for the religion of the churches. Streets around St James' knew well the sound of the carpenter's hammer and the stonemason's chisel, as houses had steadily been appearing on each side of Division Street, Union Street and Barrie Street. Early in 1884, for example, George Comer, a ship's purser, bought a lot on Division Street, built a brick house and moved in on April 18.[5]

But not only homes and the church were expanding. Queen's College was also making its presence felt in the same neighbourhood. Some children of St James' parishioners attended Queen's — often starting their studies at fourteen years of age — professors from Queen's attended St James' members, of the church were active on the council of the College, Queen's gave an honorary doctorate to the rector, and the famous principal George Munro Grant was invited to speak at more than one function at the church. Stuart's slums were a slowly fading memory. Queen's Campus was starting to take shape in earnest.

The Comer Family

Although not much is known about his origins, John Comer moved to Kingston in 1849. He came with his Irish wife and five children. Previously a storekeeper with Her Majesty's Commissariat Department in Niagara, he may have come to Kingston because of ill health. Earlier the same year he had been "ordered to Grosse Île" quarantine camp on the St Lawrence, near Quebec City. That could only mean one thing, that he was at least suspected of having typhus. Presumably he was declared clear of disease, so that he could relocate in Kingston. He joined St James' and within a few years was identified with the resolution deploring Givens' wearing the surplice.

George Comer was nine in 1849, and he attended the grammar school along with Francis Kirkpatrick who became his friend. On leaving school at fourteen he apprenticed to a printer and after various jobs in Canada and the United States settled in Kingston. Winters found him printing and book keeping; while the lakes were open he sailed as purser on several steamships including the "Corinthian" and the "Algerian." The latter, curiously enough, was none other than the refurbished "Kingston" that had carried the Prince of Wales on his abortive trip up the St Lawrence in 1860!

The Comer Family Scrapbook

George Comer, aged nine, the year he arrived in Kingston (1849).

The Whig-Standard

WEDNESDAY, OCTOBER 24,

On Sunday last, Mr. George Comer, Division street, celebrated his eighty-eighth birthday anniversary. Greetings and congratulations were received from many friends in the city and outside places. Although Mr. Comer has not been in the best of health lately, he was able to attend service that day at St. James' church, where he has been a member of the congregation for nearly eighty years.

Elizabeth Comer in 1870

KINGSTON, C. W., JUVENILE TEMPERANCE CIRCLE

PLEDGE.

We Promise that we will not Make, Buy, Sell, or Use as a Beverage, any Spirituous or Malt Liquors, Wine, o Cider; nor use Tobacco in any Form.

This is to Certify that *William Henry Comer* is a Member of this Circle, having subscribed to its Pledge.

The Comer family tableau in 1883. From left, Jessie, George, Charles, Cassa, George Junior and Elizabeth.

George Comer's teenage temperance pledge, 1855.

The steamship "Algerian" on which George Comer was purser. It was the refurbished "City of Kingston" from the 1860 fiasco described in chapter two.

George Comer in 1863.

George Comer on duty as a Custom House "preventative officer" near Gananoque, 1898.

A ticket to Toronto on the steamship 'Algerian' when George Comer was purser.

"Maple Home", 80 Division Street, the Comer house, built 1884 (photo 1995, Abi Lyon).

In 1869 Comer married Elizabeth Charles of Maple Hill Farm, Wolfe Island and the following year their first son, Charles, was born. In 1873 he bought a Gore Street house, where the next three children, including Jessie, were born. Ten years later he bought the Division Street plot, and built "Maple Home," Bessie Maple Comer's birthplace. He helped John Rayner re-instal the organ after it had been dismantled for the 1888 rebuilding. Then in 1891 he was appointed by Sir John A. Macdonald as a preventive officer in the custom's department. George Comer lived to a ripe 89 years, well beyond several family members.

The family attended St James' where the children went through Sunday School and young people's organizations, the choir, WA and so on. The best-remembered members, who after World War II were known affectionately as "Aunt Bessie" and "Aunt Jessie" (later, "antique Jessie") were prominent and colourful sisters in the congregation. In their later years they had what some saw as a visceral objection to any change, but they were ever faithful and loyal, if outspoken. Their reasons for maintaining tradition probably had much to do with their staunch anti-Catholicism. Their sincerity of personal faith and their warm hospitality is recalled by all who knew them. In 1982 Bessie died in the home where she was born. The family is remembered in a stained glass window on the west side of the building.

SEATING, SPIRITUALITY AND SOCIAL LIFE

The creation of more seating spaces reflected both the simple sense that there was insufficient room for everyone who wished to attend, and confidence in the future of the church. The Dominion of Canada was *God's* dominion, and Jesus, they believed, was busy building the church through his people. The centrality of the churches to national and local life was just taken-for-granted. St James' building, on the Arch-Union corner, was symbolic of this. The neo-gothic tower — along with the circular one of Chalmer's and the soaring one of St Mary's — cast a shadow of influence over the whole social life of Stuartville.

In 1892 statistics showed there were 5,030 Anglicans in Kingston, 5,185 Roman Catholics, while Methodists moving to the city from the country brought their numbers to 1,983.[6] Part of the growth was due to immigration, as this quote reveals: "As a fact, Anglicans coming to Kingston cannot procure a church sitting and it has fallen to the lot of St James' (under providential care) to supply the want."[7] In 1900, it was reported that the total number of St James' parish households had climbed from 225 to 241. There were usually more women than men at the actual services, although on one Sunday very heavy rain reversed the normal gender balance![8]

Despite the growth, real and apparent, St James' still fell to heartsearching when census returns showed little expansion of Anglican

Renovations to the original interior of St James', 1884.

churches in the twenty years to 1901. "Is it our machinery at fault?" they asked, "Does our inability to quite cover the ground explain the leakage? Are we putting ourselves out of touch with the people by a half-hearted cooperation in proposed schemes of moral and social reform? Or do we all need a richer baptism in the Holy Ghost?" A few months later emigration to the Canadian West was also proposed as an explanation.[9] On another occasion the magazine consoled parishioners with the news that at least a higher proportion attended church in Stuartville than in Liverpool, England or Aberdeen, Scotland![10]

Such discussions probably seemed somewhat academic to the majority of the congregation, whose lives were bound up with the rhythms of weekly activity connected with the church. Central to these was worship, twice per Sunday, at 11.00 a.m. and 7.00 p.m., with communion now being celebrated each week. This last was quite an innovation. As they had worked towards it in the 1880s, the "well-known English non-conformist" Charles Spurgeon was quoted to the effect that despite the Tractarians' "erroneous notions" about communion, the benefits of *frequency* was one thing that could be learned from them.[11]

Even before World War I, Sunday attendances began to drop off somewhat in the summer months, calling forth messages from the rector to the effect that people should seek first the kingdom of God and recall that Sunday should not be a "day of amusement."[12] Sabbatarianism

was still strong. One unbearably hot Sunday in the 1890s, when the rector himself suggested closing up, he received an anonymous postcard objecting to the idea with the comment "it will be hotter in hell"![13]

Sunday Schools met at 9.00 a.m. and 3.00 p.m., where serious, examined learning took place. In 1900 Sunday School attendance was already around 300, climbing to a pre-war peak of about 400! (See graph in appendix 1.) There were sometimes 17 or 20 teachers. The Sunday School comprised children of parishioners plus some who lived in the Orphan Home built near the corner of Union and Gordon (University) in 1862.[14]

Teachers met to consider what methods were most appropriate and to plan their teaching strategies. They felt they had to compensate for the declining levels of religious instruction in schools. In local high schools and collegiate institutes students could fail on questions as simple as who was Jacob's youngest son or the first Christian martyr.[15] One person who helped Sunday School teachers think about how they taught was a member of the St James' congregation, William Stewart Ellis, principal of Kingston Collegiate Institute.[16] Ellis went on to pioneer vocational education in Ontario and to become dean of the Education Faculty at Queen's.

A weekday Bible study meeting happened each Wednesday at 7.00 p.m. and a service was held in the jail at 2.00 p.m. Sunday. Prayer Book services included sung sections led by the choir, of which St James' people were already proud, and the centrepiece seems to have been the sermon, always derived from and sticking close to the biblical text. Presumably the building alterations brought the choir into the chancel (it had previously sung where the 1854 organ was played, in the gallery).

The fact that a prayer meeting was held on Wednesday evenings does not necessarily mean that the room was packed with praying people. In 1891, for instance, Rector McMorine saw the "meagre attendance" as a "pitiable commentary on the religious life of the congregation. Is it possible — he went on — that the handful of people in the school room represents the sum total of those who regard it as a duty or esteem it as a privilege to devote an hour in the week to public prayer and praise?"[17]

The same people who worshipped together also met in numerous other church-related contexts. These laity-led groups flourished for several decades, especially from the 1880s to the 1930s. Most important were the Temperance Society and the Woman's Auxiliary, which started life in 1885 and included some "Dorcas work" that is, sewing. By the turn of the century, in addition to the Woman's Auxiliary there was a Girl's Auxiliary, the Church Children's Missionary Guild, Ladies' Aid, the Anglican Young People's Association, the Brotherhood of St Andrew, the Young Men's Club and the Scripture Reading Union.[18] Even the Young People's Scripture Union could boast, in 1903, of 147 turning out for a talk on the history of the Bible.

William H. Ellis, St James' member and principal of Kingston Collegiate Institute c. 1912 (courtesy KCVI).

Orphans' home, built 1862, destroyed by fire 1947. For many years, children from the house attended St James' Sunday School. The John Deutsch University Centre now stands on the site.

And the list goes on! In 1898 a Boy's Brigade was organized, to run bi-weekly. They wore khaki, and because of his military background the Rev G.L. Starr was the "officer" in charge.[19] In addition there were groups for sports activities, whose number was to grow in the first part of the twentieth century. These groups each had their special events, but there were also excursions and garden parties that involved much larger numbers.

Each Christmas "Children's Treats" were mounted, including recitations, music and "humour." In the summertime a whole raft of activities was available; strawberry socials (what "toothsome fruits" exclaimed the church magazine!), garden parties, moonlight steamship trips to Gananoque, a Grand Trunk Railway outing to Ottawa or a KP&CEC streetcar ride to Lake Ontario Park and, most usually, daytime steamer trips to an island for a picnic and games. In the 1880s Channel Grove (near what is now the winter ferry dock on Wolfe Island) was the favourite destination. For super-special occasions these could include music from a military band!

In short, social life in Stuartville at the turn of the century revolved around the church. St James' was not the only church, and was not atypical. Weekly worship, the marking of special life-moments of birth, marriage and death, involvement in groups for evangelism, missionary support, music, sport, crafts, social welfare and education all occurred in the church context. Social life was focussed locally in the Stuartville neighbourhood, and this was further emphasised by the fact that excursions to the islands or to towns like Ottawa were so special and well-attended.

"The annual Sunday School excursion took place on July 30th [1886] and was attended by 400 persons, 130 being adults. The boat had only just left when it was discovered that the boxes of provisions had been left forgotten on the wharf. Mr Rogers [the lawyer] kindly offered to return to the city and bring them back as best he could. Meanwhile a telegram was sent from Garden Island and Mr Toye, confectioner, and the affable railway manager, B.W. Folger promptly hired the steam yacht "Juno" and surprised the picnickers by arriving with supplies in advance of anticipations. Races, games and a bountiful tea followed in due course. The "Pierrepont" returned about 8.00 p.m. and the party having been got on board with some difficulty, returned to Kingston in high glee. The funds of the Sunday School were benefitted to the amount of $10.80." (From a report in Home Words.)

KINGSTON, A SLOW STARTER

The occupational make-up of the St James' congregation, plus the nature of the excursions, gives some clues about the kind of place Kingston

The "Pierrepont" docked in front of City Hall. St James' rented this steamer for outings: it also functioned as a Wolfe Island ferry. (Marine Museum of the Great Lakes Archive).

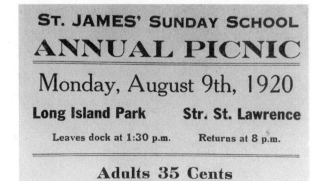

ST. JAMES' SUNDAY SCHOOL
ANNUAL PICNIC
Monday, August 9th, 1920
Long Island Park   Str. St. Lawrence
Leaves dock at 1:30 p.m.   Returns at 8 p.m.

Adults 35 Cents

The steamship outings continued until well into the twentieth century.

Advertisements from the St James' *Home Words* magazine, December, 1888, show the businesses of several members.

was at the turn of the century. Some military personnel still attended, plus those associated with the ships and wharves on the waterfront. Others were small traders, plus doctors, lawyers and teachers. (The most prominent lawyer, Robert Rogers, helped people keep up with the times in his book on "Rights and Wrongs of a Traveller, by Boat, by Stage, by Rail."[20]) Because the parish was thought of geographically, a mixed crowd came to church each week, and the congregation was certainly not skewed towards students even though Queen's was expanding.

Kingston was growing at a rate far slower than other Ontario cities like Ottawa, Hamilton and Toronto. The 1881 population of 14,091 had risen to 19,263 by 1891 but actually declined again by 1,302 by 1901. Although the transshipment trade had been steady, it was already failing and did not attract population as other centres did. Kingston's experiments in manufacturing — both ships and locomotives — also met with only limited success. No wonder Kingston was known to its critics as "sleepy hollow," a "land where it is always afternoon."[21]

Nonetheless, St James' people were both users of and workers in transport industries. The Kingston Street Railway Company was founded in 1877, and on weekdays one must have heard from St James' the screech of steel on steel as cars rounded the corner of Barrie and Union. In 1893 the streetcar was electrified (with the further potential of being run on ammonia or compressed air if these were agreed to![22]). This increased its attraction as the acme of modern transport, and the Sunday School certainly enjoyed using it for their 1895 summer excursion to Lake Ontario Park, the terminus, and no doubt on other occasions as well.[23]

For turn-of-the-century Ontario Protestants the street cars could also pose a threat to a precious institution, the work-free Sunday. Observing the Lord's Day was a key practice, symbolizing God's dominion over all life.[24] This was recognised at St James' as much as anywhere, where Lord's Day Alliance speakers were welcome, and where encouragement was given to observe the new Lord's Day Act.[25] Controversy peaked in July 1911 when the street car company went ahead with plans for Sunday trips to Lake Ontario Park, despite vociferous resistance from the Lord's Day Alliance. The company tried to placate objectors with the promise of no "questionable" amusements and nothing being sold in the park and it seems they won the day. 4100 adults and as many children took advantage of the first Sunday trips.[26]

Like other Kingstonians, St James' people were still involved in water-related businesses around the turn of the century. Charles Crysler, "a constant worshipper at St James'" is an example. He commanded Lake Ontario steamships all

his life, until five years before he retired, when he became the Inspector of Weights and Measures for Kingston. George Comer worked on Great Lakes shipping routes until he became a customs officer in 1891. In 1902 the steamer "Bannockburn" left Fort William (now Thunder Bay) on November 21 and was never seen again. Five of the missing crew were associated with St James', including an engineer, a wheelsman and a watchman.[27]

Other St James' people were well known in public life. The best example is Edward Pense, who was a warden from 1877–1882 and again from 1886–1895. He had worked from his youth at *The British Whig*, his grandfather Edward Barker's daily newspaper. After being junior clerk, reporter, proofreader and business manager her took over the paper at age twenty-four in 1872. He expanded the business, taking advantage of the latest new printing technologies, and under him the *Whig* moved to the premises it has today. But he could claim that "No man ever left the office on Saturday night without the full amount of his wages, even if it were necessary to spoil the Egyptians."[28]

Pense became a Frontenac Ward alderman in 1876, and was elected at age thirty-three, in 1881, the youngest-yet mayor of Kingston. He became president of the Canadian Press Association the same year. In 1901, 1902 and 1905 he was Liberal member of the Provincial Parliament. Of the issues that engaged him, prohibition came near the top of the list. A member of the St James' Temperance Society, his religious views made him a moderate prohibitionist, and also influenced his politics in other ways. He was well-liked by most Kingstonians, and had a secure reputation elsewhere. The Toronto *Globe* regretted his losing the parliamentary seat in 1908, while the Stratford *Beacon* said he was "at once one of the ablest and most upright men in Canadian journalism."[29]

For many decades the bell in St James' tower rang out before services and for weddings and funerals. It also sounded the community fire alarm for a while! In 1893 a new bell was installed in memory of Rybert Kent who had lived at Sunnyside on Union Street, and then at 85, King Street. This bell was cast at the Meneely Company, an Irish family firm in West Troy, New York.[30]

Old Stuartville — unlike Kingston itself — at the turn-of-the-century was a growth area. Transient, unskilled labour was largely a thing of the past, as was the heavy concentration of taverns. Homes, workshops and stores were established. Robert Hendry's chandlery business supplied shipbuilders from Earl and Barrie, and Alexander Adair's grocery store stood on the Barrie-Agnew (William) corner. Limestone buildings of the capital era gave way to the brick or frame houses of Stuartville where families lived, children were raised and where the nodes of social networks were churches.

THE CAMPUS CREEPS CLOSER

By 1899 Queen's had six hundred students on campus. The earliest buildings were the ones closest to St James'; Summerhill and the Old Medical Building. Although new facilities had appeared, the Arts Building, the Science Building, and Carruthers Hall, space was still at a premium. Kingston Hall dated from 1900, into which the arts faculty moved in the fall of 1902. In the same year, foundation stones were laid for Ontario Hall (for the School of Mining) and Fleming Hall. They were completed in 1903, followed by Grant Hall in 1904. This spate of building continued before the First World War with the erection of Nicol Hall and Gordon Hall, for the School of Mines on Union Street.[31] Thus the physical presence and proximity of Queen's became more and more apparent to local parishioners.

Of course, the campus was even more open and spacious than today. The buildings were at the edge of a very large green court[32] which gave the campus a semi-rural look. Indeed, in the 1890s the janitor's cow still grazed below Summerhill, between the cabbage patch and the muddy stream that ran across towards the hospital from Arch Street.[33] Perhaps this is the pasture that Kirkpatrick's son would later recall playing on as a child.

The growth of Queen's in those years was largely the result of the vision and tremendous energy of Principal George Grant. The university was steadily establishing itself as a national institution, and moves were afoot at the turn of the century to cut the denominational ties with the Presbyterian Church. This did not mean, however, that Queen's was becoming "secular" in the sense that it was forsaking religious commitments or debate. Far from it! Grant's own activities as a confessing evangelical who simultaneously was a passionate believer in free inquiry saw to that!

Grant was not afraid to complain about hypocrisy and complacency in the churches, and was especially scathing about a Christianity that was not life- and society-changing. As we saw in the previous chapter, he encouraged the founding of the Alumni Theological Conference in 1893, that gave the opportunity for discussion of modern ideas of biblical criticism and social Christianity. But while he remained convinced that ethics should be rooted in "the fact of evil and the necessity of divine redemption," it was just this conviction which conference participants would increasingly question.

Enlightenment confidence in the "goodness of man," a blurring of the category "Christian" and the sowing of seeds of doubt regarding the trustworthiness of the Bible would eventually produce the secular outcome that was the opposite of Grant's intentions.[34] None of this can have escaped the attention of St James' although the full implications of these shifts only revealed themselves gradually.

Ongoing and cordial connections between St James' and Queen's included the church using Queen's facilities from time-to-time for special events, and the fact that the church supplied both students and professors for the university. Robert Vashon Rogers, for instance, both continued his father's work as a loyal St James' member, served Queen's on the University Council [35] and, when the law faculty was revived in 1888, as a professor.[36] In 1890 he was involved in the unsuccessful bid to keep the Women's Medical College open, only a few years after the initial controversy over whether women should study medicine at all.[37]

St James' saw the Queen's campus as part of its mission. The Brotherhood of St Andrew, for instance, which was essentially an evangelistic movement, tried to attract Queen's students. Just before Christmas in 1899, they issued an invitation to Queen's men for a social, with "music and recitations" though perhaps the real attraction was "the gramaphone."[38] It is noted in particular that the rector, McMorine (also a council member at Queen's) was a "friend and confidant" of students, which suggests that St James' was already making its mark as a student-oriented church.

At the installation of Principal Gordon in 1903, Queen's gave McMorine an honorary doctorate. He shared the honour with Salem Bland, the Social Gospeller, Nathaniel Burwash, Methodist founder of Victoria University in Toronto, K.J. Cody of Wycliffe College, G.W. Ross, premier of Ontario, and several others, including fellow Kingstonians Malcolm Macgillivray of Chalmers and John Mackie of St Andrew's. The dinner conversation must have been fascinating!

| A pre-World War I postcard of St James.

SOLEMNITY AND JUBILATION

Few *fin-de-siècle* fears bothered Kingstonians or Canadians. A strong and positive sense of purpose was evident. Sir Wilfrid Laurier went to Britain for Queen Victoria's jubilee in 1897; the empire was flourishing. Gold was found in the Klondike which sent prospectors streaming west and north. (St James' had its stake there, too; a missionary, W.G. Lyon, who was killed in a canoe accident in 1898.[39]) Even the Boer War, far from dampening spirits, was hyped up in Kingston by the military presence and by groups like the Loyal Orange Lodge and the Imperial Order of Daughters of the Empire. General optimism was reflected in Wilfrid Laurier's famous comment that the twentieth century would be "Canada's century."

The churches were the backbone of Canadian society. They were the centre of the social lives of most people. This was especially true of churches like St James' that encouraged the active involvement of all in numerous groups and societies as well as in weekly worship and Sunday School. Men led the vestry meetings, sent delegates to synod and oversaw many practical duties in the church. Women worked in their groups to provide help for the poor and to raise funds for both local and faraway missionary work. John McMorine was president of the Temperance Society, Edith McMorine president of the Woman's Auxiliary and Julia McMorine president of the Young People's Guild. Robert Rogers junior

The robed and capped choir appear with white-bearded rector MacMorine and his vicar, Thomas Savery, in December 1909 (*Parish Magazine).*

was president of the Brotherhood of St Andrew.

1893 was the year when the Anglican Church of Canada created its own General Synod and took responsibility for its own Prayer Book, while still looking over its shoulder to the parent church in Britain. Its leaders signed a "Solemn Declaration," printed at the front of all the unrevised Prayer Books, pledging allegiance to the Thirty-Nine Articles of the Church of England, the classic creeds and, of course, to the old prayer book itself. The Solemn Declaration was a landmark that no one would try to move for many decades.

In 1895 St James' celebrated its first fifty years, in fine style. They looked back on God's evident goodness to the church and looked forward confidently to the future. Festive events included a parochial reunion at the YMCA, tea and entertainment for children and young people, "musical services by full choir," and an address by Judge MacDonald of Brockville on "the duty of Christians generally to Christian life and service."[40]

During the actual services tribute was paid again to the first two rectors and "bright hymns" were sung. These included Kirkpatrick's favourite, that seems to have been a special occasion standard at St James': "Jesus, I am resting, resting, in the joy of what Thou art." The text of the sermon was 1 Corinthians 1:18, "For the message of the cross is foolishness to those who are perishing, but to us who are being saved it is the power of God."[41]

For many decades an oft-quoted hymn — sung at Kirkpatrick's funeral and the 1895 Jubilee alike — was this:

> *Jesus, I am resting, resting in the joy of what Thou art;*
> *I am finding out the greatness of thy loving heart.*
> *Thou hast bid me gaze upon Thee,*
> *And thy beauty fills my soul,*
> *For, by thy transforming power,*
> *Thou hast made me whole.*

Jean Sophia Pigott (1840-82)

ALL SEATS IN THIS CHURCH
ARE FREE.

The Church is maintained solely
by the voluntary offerings
of its people.

All Members of the Congregation
are invited to support their
Church through the Weekly
Envelope System.

NOTE: Seats will be assigned, as far as possible, by the Wardens to
all Members of the Congregation so desiring.

This notice presumably appeared when
pew rents were finally abolished in
1913. An envelope system for Sunday
giving began in the late 1890s, the
income from which almost matched
pew rent by 1900.

Turn-of-the-century view of
the chancel.

Semi-Centennial Festival
leaflet, 1895.

A view of the Kingston waterfront
taken from Edward Pense's *A Souvenir
of Kingston*, 1906 (Lorne Pierce
Collection, Queen's).

PROFILE
JOHN KERR MCMORINE
RECTOR 1885–1909

John Kerr McMorine[42] was born in the thriving textile village of Ramsay, near Almonte, Ontario, in 1842. He was the son of a Presbyterian minister, also named John, who sailed from Scotland to Canada in 1837 after graduating in theology from Edinburgh. Young John apparently loved to be outdoors, studying botany first hand in the woods behind the manse. He attended school, which was supplemented with learning Latin and Greek from his father.

At age fourteen he started at Queen's on a ten-pound Trustee Scholarship — his father was the trustee — where he received several prizes, not surprisingly in Greek, Latin, Natural Philosophy and Math. He was one of ten graduating BA in 1859, but continued in theology, and then to his MA, which he received in 1863 for a thesis on "War: its causes and consequences." Ordained June 15 1864, he worked first for Renfrew Presbytery as a missionary to Bromley, with a congregation still meeting in homes.

For reasons that are not clear,[43] McMorine came rather quickly to alter his views on how biblical was the Presbyterian way, switching to the "Episcopal" church. Records next show him as a deacon in Lanark, where he became parish priest in 1869. He had married Edith Meyer in 1868, and during his first year in Lanark his first son, John, was born. John senior continued to

John Kerr McMorine when he became rector, 1885.

study during the winters at Queen's. From 1870-1877 he was with St Paul's church in the booming manufacturing town of Almonte, though he found this place "too civilized" for his "pioneering spirit."

This restlessness and spirit of adventure took him to a Thunder Bay mission post in the following year, headquartered at Arthur's Landing. This work was obviously more to his liking, and he thrived on it, extending the ministry to Fort William, Oliver Township and Silver Islet, which he reached by boat or by crossing the Thunder Bay ice. A man of "vigorous health," he walked the 16 miles across swamps and rough trails to Oliver once a month, taking services and visiting parishioners before returning three days later. In winter he used snowshoes given him by an Indian friend.

They faced considerable difficulties, especially when the Arthur's Landing church building and rectory burned. But in these "trying years . . . the rector and his wife were knit together with their people in close bonds of mutual respect." Once the Arthur's Landing church had their meeting place restored, and with the construction of a little church building in Oliver, McMorine felt that his work in the area was sufficiently complete to accept the call to St James' Kingston in 1885.[44]

The McMorine family filled the rectory with the sound of children's games. The seven children (excluding the last, Kate, who died in infancy) grew up there, attending local schools and Queen's.[45] John and Edna were frugal parents, (who apparently took their task very seriously; McMorine once gave a synod talk on "Parental Responsibility") and one imagines the children enjoyed happy times in the rectory. The snowshoes stood in the hallway, and McMorine was a constant source of stories about Thunder Bay mission adventures. He was said to have had a "gentle spirit and dry wit" and to have been "a delightful conversationalist." The blow of their invalid son John's death at age 21 must have been very hard to bear.

What was McMorine's ministry like? His sermons, characterised by the "power to clothe words in graphic and poetic language," appealed to many. He also encouraged concern for missions elsewhere, no doubt in part from his personal experience. One report states that "Mr McMorine's pastorate is the story of continual, earnest endeavour, backed up by a loyal, sympathetic and zealous congregation, working for the building up of the Kingdom of God in the district for which he and they were primarily responsible, and in the great world beyond whose need of the gospel was ever before the people, so that St James' became known for its missionary spirit."[46]

Some felt it necessary to remind him from time to time of the Protestant character of St James'. It is possible that the subtler Anglican nuances would not have been immediately evident to someone from a Presbyterian background. When someone wanted to instal the old "papist" symbols in the chancel he was warned that things like credence tables were "illegal, unnecessary" and would "be a cause of dissatisfaction to other members of the congregation."[47]

He clearly won the confidence of the diocese, because he was appointed, successively, Rural Dean of Frontenac, Canon of St George's Cathedral, and Archdeacon of Ontario. He chaired the Synod Committee on the State and the Church, apparently delighting Synod meetings with his reports.

In later years McMorine suffered from chronic bronchitis, which meant he had to take extensive holidays, often further South. His daughter Mildred cared for him after Edith died in 1898, and he retired from active parish life in 1909. He died in Georgia, where he was wintering, on November 24, 1912 and he was buried in Cataraqui Cemetery.[48]

John Kerr McMorine in later life, c. 1907.

5

The Great World Beyond

"Nearer and nearer draws the time — the time that shall surely be
When the earth shall be filled with the glory of God as the waters cover the sea"
— Arthur Ainger[1]

Every few months, for many years, a bale of clothing, blankets and other supplies was packed and dispatched from St James', bound for destinations as close as Northern Ontario and as far away as India or Japan. Most of those making or mending the clothes or purchasing and collecting together goods in linen and wool were women; the packers included men. This was no mere aid agency. It was seen as no less than "extending the kingdom of God."

St James' Church was concerned not only for its own immediate neighbourhood, but also the "great world beyond." This phrase, used by a contemporary observer at the end of McMorine's twenty-four year stint as rector, indicates broader horizons than Stuartville, both across the continent and overseas. The bales were regularly dispatched as concrete expressions of support, in addition to personnel and prayer, for missions outside Kingston. St James', which itself had begun as a mission-supported church (of the Society for the Propagation of the Gospel), turned within a generation into a mission-supporting church.

The last decades of the nineteenth century and the first ones of the twentieth were marked by huge missionary expansion from Western Christian churches. Revivalism helped spur the movement and new trade-and-transport routes made it feasible. Canada was a leader in this movement and among local congregations St James' was certainly among the most active, enthusiastic and committed. Giving to missions at St James' did not, however, routinely outstrip the giving of other congregations. The churches in Belleville and Brockville sometimes surpassed St James' in this way.

Three dimensions of mission work may be discerned: native and immigrant home missions, and overseas missions. The diocese of Ontario, and St James', were concerned primarily with the first and third.

Chronologically, this chapter overlaps in part with the previous one, taking us from McMorine's ministry (1885–1912) and into Thomas Savery's (1912–1930). The life story of the latter appears after this chapter. Missionary outreach and expansion was taking place among the many other activities of the later nineteenth century church and well into the twentieth century.

This part of the St James' story focuses less on what happened in Stuartville and more on how local life was connected, continentally and globally, with the wider church. But in fact the forms of connection are worth noting. One is the agencies that served to find potential missionaries, to train them, and to locate them in the field. But the other form of connection involves looking at who, exactly, were the most significant players.

Both the local links, and sometimes the missionaries themselves, were women. Such women were the backbone of fundraising, and also must have known most about distant lands. Alice Hague of India, one of the first graduates of the deaconess programme at Wycliffe College, was for a long time a well-loved St James' missionary.

A WOMAN'S PLACE

In the last two decades of the nineteenth century St James' showed much interest in the work of the Church of England Zenana Missionary Society. "Zenana," explained a visiting representative, Miss Ling, to a crowd gathered at St George's in 1889, means "woman's place." Ling lived in Madras and more recently in the Nilgiri Hills, bringing the Christian message to high caste Indian women. These "Hindoos and Mahommedans" were secluded in their apartments, married young, and suffered great abuse from their husbands. At another similar meeting, the "degradation and extreme subordination of women was graphically illustrated, as well as a steady increase in the gospel of Christ."[2]

Victorian Christianity was seen to have a civilizing influence, in which women often had a central role. The culture brought by missionaries was clearly a preferable one to that of its recipients. The gospel expressed itself practically through literacy, education, political reform and, in this case, through ameliorating the situation of oppressed women. By and large, the religious outlook and practices of people to whom missions were sent were seen as the root cause of corruption, inequality and unhappiness. Thus the truth that Christianity may have positive cultural effects was compromised by the assumption that Christianity spelled Western culture.

Women were pivotal to the missionary

expansion of St James' and of Canadian church-es in general. At a time when opportunities for official, ordained leadership were non-existent (within Anglican churches, that is), women were at the forefront of missions, at home and abroad. They raised funds energetically, and often used them to support female missionaries. Professional outlets for medicine, administration and teaching opened abroad while remaining closed at home.[3] Male leaders such as Thomas O'Meara, of Little Trinity, Toronto, and later, Wycliffe College, actively encouraged women's ministry.[4]

The term "woman's auxiliary" may suggest that women were in a secondary role within mis-sionary endeavour. Nothing could be further from the truth. One route to women eventually finding their "place" in Christian leadership was through their indispensable role working in and for missions. It has been suggested that in Ulster, evangelicalism was more important than femi-nism for enlarging women's sphere of action in the nineteenth century. This may well also be true for Ontario.[5] While women's activities were still in some ways circumscribed by men, mis-sions and other activities gave women opportu-nities well beyond their traditional spheres.

BEYOND KINGSTON

From the 1880s onward St James' bales were sent to different parts of Canada, including Somerset, Manitoba, the Peigan Reserve in Fort McLeod, Alberta, Algoma, Portage la Prairie, and Wabuskang, Rupertsland. Clothing and other goods were sent with poverty, and especially child poverty in mind.[6] But the bales were sent to Christian workers on the reserves, workers who were establishing churches, schools, farms and workshops.

The idea of bringing the Christian gospel to native peoples was not new. French Catholics, after all, had been involved since the mid-six-teenth century. Locally, the first Mowhawk set-tlers in Upper Canada were Loyalists and were already part of the church. John Stuart, having been a missionary to Mohawks himself, contin-ued to be thoroughly committed to them when rector of St George's, Kingston. He and Joseph Brant (c.1742–1807 — Molly Brant's brother) translated Mark's Gospel into Mohawk, and he was intimately involved in providing buildings, catechists and teachers for them. Methodists as well as Anglicans had a good rapport with the Mowhawks in particular.

Bishop Charles Stewart of Quebec, who had welcomed Robert Rogers to Canada when he came from Ohio, had been, like Rogers, a travel-ling missionary. In 1830 he founded "the Society for Converting and Civilizing the Indians and Propagating the Gospel among Destitute Settlers in Upper Canada." The "civilizing" policy was pursued especially in the educational projects of its missions, such as that to the Ojibway of Manitoulin Island, led by Charles Brough and latterly by Irish immigrant Frederick O'Meara.[7] British groups such as the Church Missionary

Society (CMS) and the SPG attracted the interest of Canadian Anglicans. But not until the founding of the Domestic and Foreign Missionary Society (DFMS) in 1883 did Canadian Anglican work with Indians begin in earnest.[8]

For the last twenty years of the nineteenth century St James' concern with Christian missions to Indians, and that of other Kingston churches, came to the fore. The Indian Act of 1876 had placed the reserves in the hands of Indian agents, but churches were prominent in offering educational and other facilities. The bales prepared by the WA went out, and letters and occasional visitors came back. Three little sketches serve to give the flavour of these contacts and, for the twentieth century, controversies.

J.G. Brick worked in Dunvegan in the Peace River district of Athabasca diocese, and visited Kingston in 1887. He spoke of "Indian character and customs and the nature of Christian work among these people." He was attempting to establish a model farm (with a government subsidy). The following year the St James' magazine reported that he now had a saw and grist mill plus some farm implements. (As an interesting aside, Brick also said he had known nothing of the North-West rebellion until it was all over. While the new Canadian Pacific railway had meant rapid defeat for the Métis, communication to nearby districts was still slow.)

The Rev and Mrs Bourne were on the Peigan Reserve near Fort McLeod Saskatchewan in the late 1880s. They struggled to erect their own log cabin while living in the school house where the Indians were taught. Jane Bourne knew she would get a positive response from St James' when it came to a request for helping with materials for their home. For one thing, St James' sent bales of clothing to them to distribute among what she called the "poor wretched Indians." For another, work among Indians was often done in competition with other Christian groups. St James' sympathies would be aroused by realising that "Romanists" were the other party at the Peigan reserve.

A request from Peigan Reserve. In 1891 a letter was received in Kingston requesting the help of the WA: ". . . for small bands of workers, I think if they would send a good supply of large, long kitchen aprons made with pockets and bibs that come up very high . . . We can never get enough stockings . . . Workbags, containing spools of cotton, coarse needles, scissors and combs would be very useful. Pictures, especially Bible illustrations, are in great demand . . . Anything that will amuse the children we will be most grateful for. Dolls, dressed or undressed, material for dressing them, games, puzzles, etc."[9]

Charlie Maggrah and Benjamin Chimgwauk from the Shingwauk School (Notman Photographic Archives, McCord Museum, Montreal).

E.F. Wilson was a well-known British (CMS) missionary among Ojibways and Blackfeet at the Shingwauk Home in Sault Ste. Marie. St James' once used prayer books printed at that home. Wilson visited Kingston in 1887, along with 28 children who billeted with local families. A presentation was made at City Hall, with drama and singing from the children, and pictures of Indian life that included a portrait of Ta-tanka I-yotank, or Sitting Bull. The St James' report commented that the sight of the children "around Mr Wilson who was instructing them in scripture truth and history [was] a loving and happy picture, suggesting thankful thoughts of the moral and spiritual elevation which Mr Wilson had been instrumental in effecting among those rude races."[10]

Another feature of missionary involvement at St James' was that the rectors would themselves visit missionaries in far-flung places. John McMorine followed this tradition, having himself been an adventurous travelling bush-parson in his younger days. There was thus plenty of scope for discovering first hand what conditions were like in other parts of the Dominion. He would visit distant places during some summers, and report back. In 1896, for instance, McMorine wrote to St James' during a visit to Portage la Prairie, describing the impoverished conditions among the Sioux bands that had escaped North from the United States.

There is no doubt that these missionary efforts were paternalistic, or that they assumed

Indian would have to give way to European and Canadian culture. On the other hand, the full situation cannot faithfully be captured with the simple stereotypes that are routinely trotted out today. People like Wilson had considerable confidence in the capacity of Indians to learn, and to participate in political life.[11] Moreover, it was leading Ontario evangelical laypeople like the Toronto lawyer "Sam" Blake who were first to question, at the turn of the twentieth century, the wisdom of taken-for-granted features of Indian work. This included doubt about residential schools, and the thought that even day schools could well be taken over by secular authorities.[12]

Serious rethinking would not take place until the 1960s, particularly with the publication of Charles Hendry's *Beyond Traplines*.[13] Though the Anglican Church of Canada explicitly acknowledged wrongs done earlier, the mixed legacy of residential schools is still controversial today. As for St James', attention turned to foreign missions long before serious doubt was entertained about the good done by the civilizing activities of those for whom prayer was made and bales were shipped.

BEYOND CANADA

St James' supported mission work abroad, right from the dawn of the Canadian missionary movement. At the turn of the century, general missionary giving accounted for around 15% of the church budget.[14] India was referred to above,

but Japan was actually the first focus of interest and support. Canadian Methodists had been working in Japan for about a decade when the first ever Canadian Anglican missionary, John Cooper Robinson, went there. He went to work in Nagoya, in the South Tokyo diocese, in 1888. Sponsored by the Wycliffe College Mission Society, and supported by the diocesan WA, he was the first of many Canadian Anglicans in Japan.[15]

Japan was opening to Western influence at this time. The Meiji Restoration of 1868 encouraged the quest for contact with others. One reason missionaries could go was the belief that Christianity's association with Western civilization would aid Japan's modernizing thrust. By the 1930s Canada had more missionaries in the Japanese Empire than any other country. Until the 1940s the only Canadians ordinary Japanese had contact with were missionaries. They were role-models not only for Christian discipleship but for Western culture.

G.J. Waller went to Japan with the newly formed DFMS in 1890 and a few years later was back in Canada, speaking at St James' about his work.[16] It seems that work in Nagano was the most closely followed at St James'. Indeed, Mrs R.V. Rogers, a St James' and a diocesan WA president, had Japanese work named for her, the "Alice Rogers Memorial Nurses' Home" in Nagano. By 1930, St James' church had her own missionary working in Japan, a Queen's graduate named Dr R.K. Start. He was supported by the

Mrs. R.V. "Alice" Rogers, WA president,
c. 1896.

Alice Hague, St James' missionary in India
c. 1926.

Welch bequest, which is dedicated to mission work.[17]

Similar long-term commitments to Christian work in India may be found in the life of St James'. The Zenana mission preoccupied the WA from its inception, and bales were sent to India routinely for many decades. Missionary interest was quickened when St James' "own" worker was abroad. Personal knowledge often increases prayer and giving in this way. Alice Hague, the first graduate of the Deaconess and Missionary Training House at Wycliffe College[18] and St James' "own" representative, worked in Kangra, India, 1912–25.

Hague's letters were always read with enthusiasm at the WA, and the church could keep contact the more easily with one who was known to them and had grown up herself through the St James' (her father was George Hague, a warden). On her return from India she continued to be part of the WA, and was made a life-member. Her presence as a retired missionary helped maintain interest in Christian work overseas.

WOMAN'S AUXILIARY

The St James' Woman's Auxiliary Group began in 1885 and would prove to be one of the strongest and longest-lasting associations in the life of the church. Of the many lay-run organizations flourishing at that time, this one was prominent for its being female-led, for having strong local ties with the diocesan WA (over which several St James' women presided) and for its intense concern for the broad mission thrust of the church. The St James' WA lasted for a century, right up to the 1980s.

The Domestic and Foreign Missionary Society came into being in 1883 and just two years later seven women approached its leaders at an Ottawa meeting, offering their services as an auxiliary to mission work.[19] It is not clear whether any of the seven was from St James' although the St James' group was a "charter member." With their motto "The love of Christ constraineth us" they dedicated themselves first to prayer. They were quite clear about this priority, which could no doubt be taken as a guide for other church activities as well.

"All branch work," they said, "should be carried on in the spirit of prayer . . . the higher the spiritual ideals of the branch, the better the work is done, and the less danger there is of the meetings becoming mere sewing circles or social gatherings."[20] By prayer, they meant, "individual and collective intercessory" prayer; specific, spoken, shared prayer for others. After this, their other concerns were sharing information about mission work, increasing mission activity, giving money, strengthening diocesan boards and encouraging *all* women in each parish to be involved.

At St James', these aims were pursued vigorously. The Dorcas Department of the WA oversaw sewing and knitting for the clothing and bedding bales. Different sections of the WA were soon meeting at different times, including one for girls. They also tried to coordinate their activities with those of the Girl Guides, the Sunday School and, when it began, the Brotherhood of St Andrew. The educational function of the WA within the church was crucial to building support for missions. This paralleled the actual work of fundraising, also undertaken primarily by the WA.

The diocesan branch of the WA evidently went through a sticky patch after ten years operation. A "sense of loss, heartache and bewilderment hung over" them at this "poignant cleavage." The incoming president in 1896, however, was St James' Alice Rogers, who, as "one who shed around her the light of a joyous Christian life" was to help pull things together again. "She had within herself all that was required for leadership to build morale, to stabilise and consolidate the depleted organization." Under her leadership, the local WA ". . . increased in stature and strength. The educational programme advanced. There was a lending library of 70 volumes all neatly covered and carefully filed at St George's Parish Hall, Kingston. The extra-cent-a-day fund was launched and a practical system of sacrificial giving was given a trial."[21]

By the turn of the century, then, the WA had established itself as a pivotal part of the church, representing prayer, giving and educational initiatives in relation to missions. It appears that some sense of partnership developed between men and women involved in mission. That mutual respect is seen for instance when at his death in

1910 Edward Pense was described as "a friend, foremost in zeal for missionary work."[22] He had been a board member of the Missionary Society of the Canadian Church (MSCC), founded 1902. Through practical forms of service, however, it was above all women who had earned the respect of men. The WA showed that women were leaders in prayer, faith and sheer hard work. They were in fact partners in mission long before they were recognised as such within the full range of Canadian church life.

THE PUZZLE PIECES

St James' played as big a role as any church in the great missionary movement that began in the last quarter of the nineteenth century. The local parish was vital as the means of securing support — prayer and money — for missions and for producing the missionary candidates. Through the work of dedicated women in the WA, considerable cooperation between St George's, St Paul's and St James' took place within Kingston, some of which may even have overlooked theological differences between them.

However, St James' missionary connection would be incomplete without mention of Wycliffe College. Enthusiasm for the evangelical seminary was clear from its birth. As we have seen, missionaries supported by St James' typically trained there. Wycliffe was founded as the Protestant Episcopal Divinity School in 1877, in an attempt to counterbalance Trinity College's high church position. Considerable conflict surrounded Wycliffe for a number of years, but this in no way inhibited its role in promoting missions. St James' obtained rectors, entertained professors, and supported missionaries from Wycliffe.

Wycliffe also encouraged women's mission involvement through the deaconess training programme. In the longer term, one wonders whether the cooling of theological disputes did not come in part through the expansion of missionary work, and through the practical partnership with women. Whatever the case, St James' involvement with the "great world beyond" was marked by the kind of keen zeal for mission of all kinds. Zeal that had once found outlets in forms of fierce Protestantism and in the temperance movement seemed increasingly to be channelled in new directions. St James' was no less Protestant or Evangelical, but its convictions were expressed in the desire for the conversion to Christ of not just Kingston or Canada, but the world.

WYCLIFFE COLLEGE

Federated with the University of Toronto

College buildings are on the University grounds and adjacent to the newly opened Hart House, the centre of the student activities of the University.

Preparation for the Christian Ministry and Foreign Mission fields in accordance with the principles of the Reformation.

COURSES LEADING TO L.Th., B.D., AND D.D

REV. CANON T. R. O'MEARA, LL.D., Principal.

H. MORTIMER, Registrar.

This advertisement appeared in the church magazine in 1924, illustrating the ongoing links between St James' and Wycliffe College.

PROFILE
THOMAS SAVERY
RECTOR 1912–1930

Thomas William Savery was born into a United Empire Loyalist family in Nova Scotia. His father, a judge, was prominent in provincial and church life. Thomas attended the County Academy at Annapolis Royal before starting at the University of Toronto and Wycliffe College in 1895. After his graduation in 1900 he was ordained deacon at St George's Kingston, by the new bishop W.L. Mills, and became curate at St James'.

In 1903 Savery went west to Winnipeg, where he was rector of St Luke's Church. He married Edna Neve, and their son, Reginald, was born in 1909. That same year he returned to St James' to assume responsibility for leadership, as vicar, on the retirement of John McMorine. He became rector when McMorine died in 1912 and his induction took place on December 22. Within three months, however, tragedy struck his own household when his wife, Edna, died, leaving him with his three-year-old son.

Not long afterwards, the Great War broke out, no doubt a further test of his own trust in God's care. Savery remarried in 1916, and he and his wife, Catherine Chute, later had two daughters, Barbara and Margaret. By the end of the war Savery was ready to put his energies into a major construction project, the parish hall built in honour of his late colleague, John McMorine.

Thomas Savery is remembered as a very kindly, gentle man. If his daughters witnessed some act of generosity he would say "Don't tell your mother." He loved to play with children and often had tricks in his pocket, like an egg that disappeared from an eggcup or a handkerchief that changed from red to blue. There were always pets in the rectory when the Savery family was there. One dog was even taught to say its prayers![23]

The 1920s found Savery busy on a number of fronts. From his involvements he clearly had an integrated view of Christian ministry, although nothing seems to have survived that gives direct evidence of his priorities. A staunch evangelical, he rejoiced to remind fellow-Anglicans of the benefits of their Reformation heritage, and he keenly supported Wycliffe College. As we shall see in the next chapter, he also welcomed opportunities to expand evangelical work among students.

In activities beyond St James' he is found, before the war, on the Diocesan Committee of Moral and Social Reform, and during the war he became president of the Kingston Evangelical Alliance. Education then featured significantly in his activities, as he worked for both the Diocesan and General Boards of Religious Education. He was a vice-president of the Children's Aid Society and first secretary to and then the appointed Rural Dean of Frontenac. He also served as president of the Kingston Ministerial Association.

Recognition for all these years of energetic activity came first in 1929 with an honorary doctorate from Queen's and then in 1930 when Savery was made a canon of St George's Cathedral. His Queen's citation said that while he was "first of all a servant of his own communion . . . his sympathies and activities have been wider than any denomination." They called him "the enthusiastic champion of all thoughtful attempts to bring together the various ecclesiastical organizations for the common good."[24]

Perhaps he felt he had done all he could in one place, because in the same year — 1930 — he was recalled to his native Nova Scotia, to become rector of St Paul's Church, the oldest Anglican church in the Dominion of Canada.

Thomas Savery, curate 1901–1903, vicar 1909–1912, rector 1912–1930

The Savery Family Scrapbook

Thomas Savery marries Catherine Chute, 1916.

Thomas Savery with his second wife, Catherine, and son Reginald, at Kingston Mills, 1919.

Thomas Savery with his wife Catherine near Kingston, 1919.

Rector Thomas Savery with daughter Barbara at their Wolfe Island cottage, 1929.

6

Peace and War

"War. . . an experience which will only create greater ill-will, greater misunderstanding that will take them farther from the face of God."

— George Grant[1]

Like any church with a long past, St James' has memorial plaques and windows to her war-dead. These reveal how deep and serious was the involvement of the parish in seeing young people leave for war-fronts overseas, and how disruptive is war in the life of any community. In the memorials you can feel the loss of families affected, and the seemingly senseless suffering through which so many went.

What the wall-mounted rolls of honour do not tell is also considerable. They give no clues as to how life went on in the parish during the wars — that annual excursions and garden parties continued, for instance — or, more importantly perhaps, how people coped with the wrench of war.

For many in Kingston it was business as usual, during both wars. In fact, a certain insulation from some of the worst effects of war is evident.

At the same time, twentieth century total war has had profound cultural effects. That modern means of transport and communication, heralded for their world-unifying potential, could be the very vehicles of mutual suspicion and slaughter is just one instance of dashed hopes. While God's name was invoked by many in both wars, George Grant may have been right to conclude that misunderstandings generated by war would take people further from God's face.

But what happened to religion in Canada is more complex than this. Peace-time events and

George Comer's rosette ribbon shows continuing Orange interest at St James'.

processes were probably just as significant as those of war. While life after World War I could largely return to a "normal" state of settled social existence, after World War II changes began to occur at a more profound social and cultural level. A new kind of consumerism would take hold, and new modes of travel and contact would make for more mobile populations. People would not necessarily move "farther from God's face," but the churches would never be the same again.

WAR AND AFTER

In the nineteenth and early twentieth centuries the churches had a profound social influence. This took a severe knock with the First War. Disillusionment about hopes for social reform followed the war experience. The internal life of the churches, though also affected by disputes over liberalism in theology, continued to be strong in the decades up to and after the Second War. St James', like any church, was touched by war and economic depression, and got involved in efforts to combat evils created by each situation, but also offered some robust responses which suggest a clarity of faith.

Anglicans, but also those in other denominations, reluctantly admitted war was a necessary evil in 1914. By the end of the war, most agreed that what actually took place was "scientific butchery."[2] However, there was a crisis, and St James' responded. Men went to the front — 399 Kingstonians volunteered within a week of war's outbreak in 1914 — and at home numerous war-time efforts began to support the allied cause. By the end of the war, 78 people had volunteered from St James'. Fourteen would never return from the front.

During the war, several groups were in action at St James', from the Armagh Club, that made bandages and hemmed towels, to Busy Bees, who made scrapbooks for men at the front, and young people's groups such as the Shrapnel Dodgers, who met for baseball and athletics. Wartime economy meant an emphasis on home dressmaking, food-saving and so on, and St James' parish was as involved as any in this.

Few were not drawn in some way or another. No one could be unaware of the crisis. Within the parish two university halls, Grant and Kingston became military hospitals, and across the Cataraqui River Fort Henry became a prison camp. Military drill was ever more evident. Depressing news of death in mud-filled trenches and strategic decisions of dubious wisdom preoccupied the papers. Passchendaele and the Somme, Vimy Ridge and Ypres were woven into local legends of loss.

When the war ended, RMC hero Billy Bishop was honoured as a flying ace — and, it seems, turned to aerial photography that included taking pictures of Stuartville and Queen's campus — the Canadian Locomotive Company reverted from shell-production to making freight engines and "conductorettes" gave their jobs back to men on the streetcar. A sense of normality slowly settled over Stuartville once more.

Sunday School teachers perhaps? Flanked by Thomas
Savery (right) and Thomas Dalby, SS Superintendant
(left), c. 1913.

The earliest available aerial photo of St James' and part of old Stuartville, attributed to Billy Bishop, 1919.

Rod Alexander, a teenager at St James', worked as a streetcar conductor 1918-1920. He collected fares — five cents when he began — but in winter he also tended the wood-burning stove in the centre of the car. The service began at 6.00 a.m. and ended at 11.00 p.m. with no regular run on Sunday. Children could go to Lake Ontario Park on summer Wednesdays for one cent! Alexander recalls the route from the market, along King Street and up Barrie Street, stopping for the hospital, round the corner onto Union Street past St James', before the Queen's stop. It continued to Portsmouth, returning along the same way as far as Alfred Street where it turned north to Princess Street and thence to the market again. One car was equipped with a snow-plough, which at the time was the only way snow was removed on Princess Street. Alexander remembers that people simply walked between the tracks when the snow was deep![3]

Champions of the Sunday School Amateur
Athletics Association c. 1910. Mr Dalby at
centre left (DOA).

It is not clear what this group is, but the photo
dates from before World War I and includes
Thomas Savery (left), William Shannon (second
from right), and William Dalby (right).

An aerial view of the Queen's campus and old
Stuartville, looking north-east (Billy Bishop,
1919, National Archives, Ottawa).

A CONSTRUCTION SITE, AGAIN

St James' in the roaring twenties remained a
hive of activity. More building took place to
facilitate the still growing range of meetings and
ministries. There would be a full-scale parish mission in 1922, for instance, and the Sunday School
grew again after the War. Perhaps the building
project also signalled a return to civilian life after
the Great War. The "McMorine Memorial Hall"
was erected and the "Rogers Memorial Chapel"
furnished in time for the 75th anniversary cele-
brations in 1920. The hall cost $30,000 to build.
A work-starting service was conducted by the
rector, Thomas Savery, and the Sunday School
organist, Miss Dupuy, turned the first sod. The
cornerstone was laid in the presence of 400.

The giving spirit of many was encouraged at
the 75th anniversary, when the bishop preached on
the text: "Then the people rejoiced, for that they
offered willingly, because with a perfect heart they
offered willingly to the Lord." Direct and relevant
preaching, it seems. The parish hall was dedicated
on the afternoon of the anniversary — October
10, 1920 — and a Children's Day Service followed. R.A. Hiltz, the General Secretary of the
General Board of Religious Education spoke on
"Responsibility," and again in the evening (which
had a harvest thanksgiving flavour) on the need for
a "true harvest" in the lives of boys and girls.

Meanwhile, work had also been under way in
the Rogers Chapel, and its refurbishment had
been completed in the Christmas week, 1919.
The building was dedicated on New Year's Eve at

| A pre-war "summer" streetcar (QUA).

From the cover of the parish magazine, 1929.
The streetcar tracks can still be seen.

a special communion service. With a great sense of the moment, they sang "For all the saints, who from their labours rest . . . " and closed with "Happy New Year" greetings at 12.30 a.m.

Their labours were not over, however. Unfortunately, a short while after its completion, cracks appeared in the east wall of the new hall, of which everyone had been so proud. Iron girders and tie rods were inserted, but to no avail. An architect condemned the wall, which had to be rebuilt, consuming another $2,600, for which the rectory had to be mortgaged. This would not be the last time that the building presented energy-absorbing challenges.

The eastern wall of the McMorine Memorial Hall, built 1920 (Abi Lyon).

In 1928 Miss Charlotte A. Dupuy was buried and with her the last living memories of the early years of St James'. Born in 1837, as a little girl she had watched the completion of the church building and the rectory, plus its various extensions and additions. Her father was H.A. Dupuy, warden from 1848-1850. She maintained a personal friendship with each of the four rectors. "The church," it was said in an appreciative note sent to her uncle when she died, "ever took a very great place in her thought and heart." The Women's Auxiliary and Sunday School kept her very busy. When Thomas Savery became rector she had a class of older girls whom she had taught since their primary days, several of whom were daughters of women for whom she had done the same thing. She also played the organ for the Wednesday evening service and the Sunday School and often organized the music for Sunday morning.[4]

A DISTANT DEPRESSION

The Great Depression years were ones of austerity, but Kingston was never as badly off as some cities. For sure, a menu worked out in Montreal in 1932 showed how a family of five could live on $4.58 a week (milk was the mainstay) and jobless men rode freightcars across the country in search of work and, sometimes, handouts. A relief camp appeared across the river at Barriefield, where such men could get bed and board, and from which the labour force was found to build the Vimy Barracks and later to refurbish Fort Henry as a tourist attraction.[5]

Kingston would no doubt have been worse off as an entirely industrial city. However, Kingston has always fulfilled a number of "sub-capital" functions, seen for instance in the Royal Military College, the penitentiaries, the asylum, which still today help stabilise the local economy. All this was more significant than any industry. No new industries appeared in the early part of the century, but existing ones — such as Kingston Shipyards, the Canadian Locomotive Company, Dominion Textile Company and the Hosiery Mill — were strengthened by the experience of war. The best waterfront land was dominated by shipping industries and railway tracks.

From the later nineteenth century until World War Two Kingston made repeated attempts to industrialise, to attract companies, seeing smokestacks as symbols of progress. But growth was sluggish compared with that of Hamilton, Toronto or Ottawa. The 1920s was the scene of major struggles over transshipment in Kingston, mainly of prairies grain.

Prescott actually won out as the Great Lakes terminus, although the Canada Steamship Lines elevator (which gave its name to Elevator Bay) in fact handled more grain than Prescott between 1930 and 1955. After World War II, the development of the St Lawrence Seaway would signal the demise of transshipment for ever. Alcan started operations in 1927, and Dupont in 1940, and although these are still large local employers, they are far from making Kingston's industry more significant than her sub-capital functions.

Kingston's changing fortunes were only partly reflected at St James. More changes to the building occurred from the mid-1920s. For the next decade, in fact, construction workers were often in evidence, and more than once the congregation had to move into temporary quarters in the McMorine Hall or Rogers Chapel. At that time, the McMorine Hall was filled with light, shafting down from the windows in the roof above. It must have made a delightful temporary sanctuary.

In 1926, under the supervision of Professor L.T. Rutledge, the chancel floor space was extended into the nave by five feet, putting the pulpit and lectern on the same level. A gothic design wainscot was put on the wall to seven feet up, a doorway was cut from chancel to chapel, the ceiling was beamed and panelled to match the nave, and furnishings stained dark walnut in keeping with the rest.

Big alterations were made in the nave, with the 1855 gallery being torn down, and the two imitation doors below being closed and plastered over. The scars of this work can still be seen today. The old choir entrance was closed and a new, wider one cut at right angles to it. Wainscotting was continued round the whole building interior and the ceiling had its ornamental beams and corbels added. The Huyck family gave three chandeliers to replace the old single one and the shades on the pillar lights were changed. Dark walnut notwithstanding, the overall effect was a lighter, brighter meeting place.

The mid-1930s saw more changes, the biggest being — after much debate — the installation of a new heating system. No doubt some workers were glad of the opportunity of work. For several years water had come in around the furnaces, the problem being the leaky roof. Shingles flew off every time there was a high wind. But the furnaces were inefficient, and a fire hazard anyway, and the one in the Rogers Chapel had collapsed completely.

Estimates showed that a steam heating system and new roof would cost $5,000, which seemed daunting to the congregation until someone offered a gift of $2,000.[6] This was enough to kick-start the project which went ahead quickly. The cost did rise, of course, to $6,500, but a debenture system plus the fundraising efforts of a new women's group, the Church Workers, meant that the work was paid for (and the rectory mortgage at last paid off) within a few years.

Keeping the building together, and ensuring that it met the needs of a changing congregation, turned out to be a constant challenge. While dedicated souls were willing to give time, money and expertise, the building was also a source of disagreement and frustration. Maintaining congregational priorities and maintaining a building sometimes prove to be contradictory tasks.

The sexton's shoulders had to be strong ones in the 1930s. Ron Campbell's son remembers: "The boiler room was at the end of a long tunnel, from the men's washroom in the basement to under the chancel area. The boiler was in a pit. To stoke the boiler my father had to reach shoulder-high to shovel coal from the coal-bin (he had a great set of arms and shoulders). The tubes in the boiler had to be punched (cleaned out) with a long brush, which was again over his head."

But the sexton's wife — Flos — also had to be strong: "I remember my mother and father with string mops washing the floor in the Sunday School Hall til the wood was near-white (all varnish gone) and then on hands and knees applying paste wax to the floor, then with a weighted polisher (approx. 8"x12") pulled and pushed over the floor . . . It looked so good when they were done."[7]

TURNING TOWARDS QUEEN'S

While Queen's was still a Presbyterian college, it seems that St James' assumed her neighbour was a partner in mission. Relations were respectful, and mutual, and continued this way right to mid-century and beyond. One important change occurred in 1912, however; Queen's had become a non-denominational university, with only the Theological College remaining explicitly Presbyterian. Perhaps this was seen as a signal of impending secularity. Although religious influences actually continued strongly for some time,[8] during the interwar years St James' began to regard Queen's in a different light, as a place *for* mission rather than a partner *in* mission.

Over the several decades since both St James' and Queen's started life, traffic had moved in both directions. Some parishioners' offspring studied at the university, and some took in students as lodgers. Some church members were employed at Queen's, as professors and in other capacities. Students attended St James' and successive rectors made work among them a priority. From the 1930s students coming for summer courses also showed up and were welcomed at St James'.[9]

Also, professors would be invited to speak at St James'. Principal Grant in particular was seen as something of an ally. He had gone with other Kingstonians to the first meeting of the Evangelical Alliance in New York as early as 1877, which locates him theologically close to St James' people, and he also came to St James' several times. His successor, Principal Gordon, spoke at

The group that inaugurated IVCF. Left to right, Pastor Ackland, Miss Thomas, female students' chaperone, Muriel David, Freddie Clough, Margaret Denton, Howard Guinness; picture taken by the 3rd student, Arthur Hill, standing on the station platform at Kingston in 1929, mailbags stacked in the rear. (Reprinted from *The Spreading Tree,* IVCF 1989, by permission).

St James' functions, for instance to the Men's Club annual banquet in February 1927. By the 1920s, more students were attending Queen's, and the close contacts continued.

Perhaps the most significant event concerning students took place when Thomas Savery heard of the coming of a young medical graduate fresh from Oxford, England, in 1929. The graduate was Howard Guinness, who had arrived in Montreal the previous fall, in response to a call issued at a British meeting of the young Christian student movement, Inter-Varsity Fellowship. It does not appear that Guinness already had contacts in Kingston, but Savery invited him to preach at St James', and Guinness met students at Queen's. The church record says he encouraged them to "band together for definite witness and definite prayer."[10] Guinness' own diary noted that "quite a number" of students were "spiritually minded, keen and true to the New Birth and the Cross."[11]

He later decided to call the students together from various universities for a conference at a camp outside Kingston in September 1929. As it happened, the venue was unsuitable, so he turned to the church that had welcomed him the year before, and arranged his conference at St James'. To his intense disappointment, only six others showed up, three of whom were "helpers" and not students at all. But they prayed together, gave the group the name of "Inter-Varsity Christian Fellowship" and elected its first president, Arthur Hill. Thus IVCF in Canada, which since has served thousands of students, with hundreds of workers, began with that event in the McMorine

Memorial Hall at St James'.[12]

The mission directed towards Queen's intensified in the 1930s. "Dr Naughton"[1] became rector in 1931. Not long after, he arranged special series of student sermons, advertised on campus, and invited various speakers to St James' to address students in particular. One such was Philip Beatty, of the Student Christian Movement. At this time, although the SCM had theologically modernist leanings, some of its members were still evangelical, so this need not be interpreted as a theological shift at St James'. In fact, for some while the SCM group met at St James' on Sunday afternoons, there were occasional SCM special services, and SCM members sometimes addressed church groups such as the WA.[14] The Naughtons also opened their home to students. Sunday afternoon tea at the rectory became quite an institution!

Dr Naughton's first series of "University Services" began on October 18 1931. Clearly a credible event, Principal W.H. Fyfe of Queen's and Dr H.A. Kent, principal of the Theological College, had been invited to read the lessons. Canon Allan P. Shatford, rector of St James' the Apostle in Montreal, was the featured speaker. He took as his topic "The Church and the University," and built on Jesus' comment that "I ever taught in the synagogue and in the temple."

The thrust of his talk is worth note. He argued that the "Author of Truth" would have regarded as "disastrous" the separation of religion and education. This "divorce" taking place at various universities (including Queen's of

Cast of "The Gypsy Rover" on the McMorine stage, 1938.

course!) could be blamed on both parties. The church "failed to take a tolerant view of arising changes and would find no place for new discoveries in science" while the universities poured unwarranted scorn on religion, looking on it as "something to be pleasantly tolerated or barred altogether as not essential."[15]

As for "setting up Theological Colleges disconnected from the University," this was "one of the greatest blunders the Church made."[16] Only "in association with a broader education" could students "properly be fitted for the ministry, to deal with the conditions and problems that confronted them." If all the university sermons were made of such strong stuff, stimulating discussions must have followed on campus and in church!

Concern for students continued to be a priority at St James', even during World War II. In fact, the first ever mission at Queen's was held in 1942, and wing-commander Gerald Gregson, a popular preacher at St James', as well as more broadly in Ontario, was the Anglican representative. Dr Naughton remarked that though this was new to Queen's, missions had been taking place for a number of years at Oxford and Cambridge in England.

AT HOME AND ABROAD

For all the pressures of the Great Depression and patent changes taking place on the Queen's campus, the impression should not be given that life at St James was all that different from that in many other parishes. During the 1920s and 1930s St James' still remained a stable centre of community life. Women in particular forged the actual links between people and place through their central role in the WA, bazaars, teas, the Sunday School and other church groups.

The congregation swelled in number, perhaps in part due to the faithful visiting of all households by the rectors.[17] The Sunday School boomed in the years from World War I to the 1930s: more than 300 children attended on average. Most parishioners lived within ten minutes walk of the building. People were baptised, married and buried at St James' and between each event, found their niche in one church activity or another.

In church people knew each other as immediate neighbours from the surrounding streets, as local transport and tradespeople and as those they met in school. Those who worshipped together also worked together in the many organizations and groups represented in the church, from the missions-oriented WA to the Boy Scouts and Girl Guides. The choir, as well as practising for Sunday services and for special Easter and Christmas music, also put on plays and musicals — Sinbad the Sailor, the Gypsy Rover, Gilbert and Sullivan — which were performed on a stage that used to be at the south end of the McMorine Hall.

Dr Naughton was keenly interested in work with children, and used his skills as a photographer to good effect. He would make lantern-slide shows, often with hand-painted slides. He would show *The Pilgrim's Progress* or the *Life of Christ* in

In the mid-1930s, Howard Campbell recalls: ". . . when a performance was to be presented we all had to help put up the steel work for the curtains, hang the curtains and make sure when you pulled the rope the curtains would open properly — this used to be a fun time just setting up. The basement area was used as dressing rooms — you usually came on stage from the east side and exited off the west side and back down the stairs to the basement."

this way. He also encouraged other activities, such as outings in summer and winter. In winter, recalls his daughter Margot, "two horse-drawn sleighs would come to the church and we would all pile on and go up Division Street, across Princess and a short way along we were in open country. . . When we got back to St James' hot cocoa and cookies were served in the church hall."

The different churches in the city cooperated with each other. Thomas Savery, for instance, had been president of the Kingston Evangelical Alliance. When he left St James' it was noted that his "close friend and co-worker in the kingdom" George Brown of Chalmers was part of the farewell proceedings. Dr Naughton later presided over the Ministerial Association. Churches continued to work together in matters of social concern, through Children's Aid, the General Hospital — as distinct from the Catholic Hotel Dieu — and so on.

The choir, October 1939, in the old Rogers' Chapel (W.J. Turnbull).

St James Guide Company approx. 1938 or 39.

At St James', missionary interest continued high, and from time-to-time letters were received from, or visits enjoyed with St James' people working in "foreign parts." Alice Hague sent letters back from India before, during, and after the Great War. When she settled back in Kingston, she helped maintain the keen missionary interest for which St James' was well known. In the later 1920s and 1930s Dr Start, working in Japan, did the same. The WA still sent regular bales, and prayer meetings continued to support such outreach at home and abroad. Many missionaries stayed at the rectory while they were in town; the Naughtons were known for their hospitality and mission interest.

In 1937, a second St James' missionary sailed for Japan, Reginald Savery,[18] newly married to Betty Rice (some were amused by the new name thus created). They worked three years in the diocese of mid-Japan before returning to Canada, where they expressed deep concern about the wartime treatment of Japanese Canadians. He worked as a chaplain in the Japanese internment camps in British Columbia — "a white Canadian who was on our side," said a Japanese internee. He was remembered as one of the "few fellow Canadians who defied the anti-Japanese tidal wave of public pressure."[19] He and his family resumed life in Japan 1952–62, with a break in Kingston and at St James' 1957–8.

In addition to the WA, St James' also spawned the so-called "Church Workers" who also supported missionaries through fundraising and prayer. They boasted an "A" and a "B"

| A pre-war choir-drama cast (?Vic Lord).

Sunday Schoolgirls
c. 1936.

| Choirboys, April 17, 1938 (G.A. Jacobs).

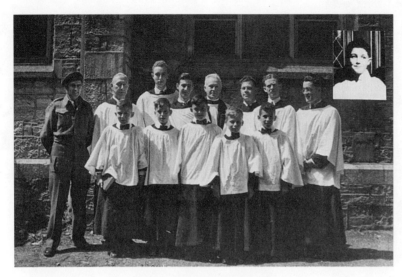

Dr Naughton with choir members during the war (DOA).

St James' Anglican Young Peoples' Association, 1948 (Vic Lord).

group, the latter of which was younger in age and almost certainly became the "Fireside Group"[20] with which the name of Eva MacKenzie-Naughton is associated. These groups collaborated to produce a wartime recipe book, called the "Victory Cookbook." The two groups continued meeting right up until the mid 1960s.

Little contact was made from St James' with the USA, and even ties with Britain began to weaken. In the later 1920s St James' stopped using the English *Home Words* magazine as the basis for parish news and switched to a Canadian source. In April 1929, St James', like many Canadian churches, responded positively to the plea that Dominion clergy encourage congregations to take Sunday seriously. The Lord's Day Alliance was commended for seeking "to preserve the Lord's Day as a day of rest against the inroads of industrialism." But the old loyalist traditions also persisted. In the 1930s Dr Naughton encouraged the Wolf Cubs at St James' to see the Bible, the Church and the King as the "three pillars of empire,"[21] and he also spoke out against the failure to acknowledge God in public life.

April 1939 saw a royal visit to Kingston. As a keen supporter of the British Empire, Dr Naughton was happy for his flock to turn out to greet king and queen, but disliked the idea of holding a service at the freshly refurbished Fort Henry. He compromised, however, by holding the St James' service earlier and by suggesting that as only 15,000 of the 100,000 expected could get into Fort Henry, they ought to "bring some of the other 85,000 to church" for the evening service! During the same visit a radio was placed by the pulpit so that the congregation could share in the dedication of the war memorial in Ottawa.

BACK TO WAR

Signs of war had been apparent for some time, but even so, when the inevitable happened it was still a shock. In the midst of the darkness and fearful apprehension, however, St James' had leaders who knew how to respond. Until hostilities actually broke out in 1939, of course, nothing altered significantly.

When the long-dreaded war began, Dr Naughton was first to acknowledge that "Britain had to keep her plighted word to Poland." But much more significantly, he commented that "Right and justice must ultimately triumph in the universe, ordered by a God of righteousness. But the cross of Jesus tells us that God himself suffers in the war against wickedness." This realistic, providential response to events issued in some gems of spirituality that made for reflective reading in the parish magazine.

"Wars solve no problems," he mused a few months later, "they only create fresh ones. The only way to a lasting peace is for the nations to walk in the way of righteousness. And it is the task of all Christian people to hold up the ideal of God's righteousness before the nations by showing forth its power in their own lives."[22] In other words, so far from either glorifying war or despairing of it, war

INEXPENSIVE WAR TIME CHOCOLATE CAKE—
Cream ⅓ cup shortening with 1 cup brown sugar. Add 1 egg unbeaten and beat hard. Mix and sift 1½ cups flour, ½ teaspoon baking powder, ¼ cup cocoa, ¼ teaspoon salt. Then add 1 cup milk and water alternately with flour mixture to the first mixture. Bake in a moderate oven.—Anonymous.

A recipe from the St James' *Victory Cookbook*, 1945.

Dr Naughton pictured in the 1930 *Year Book* (DOA).

should be seen as a spur to true discipleship.

Dr Naughton continued to stress Christian priorities throughout the war years. He himself was chaplain to the Princess of Wales Own Regiment, where he exercised a much-appreciated ministry. Soldiers were entertained in the Parish Hall and strong encouragement was given to help refugees. St James' lists 77 members who volunteered "For King and Country" in World War II. Of these, 69 returned to Kingston for civilian life. While a number of St James' members were away at war, Eva Naughton, regarded by many as the caring heart of St James', turned a group of "church workers" into the "fireside group" of women whose partners were absent. This fellowship continued into the 1950s, long after its initial purpose had been served. Eva Naughton's pastoral partnership with her husband was crucial during the dark days of war.

But Dr Naughton knew these activities, though vital, were not enough on their own. He wanted to impress the need for spiritual concerns to be yoked with the tangible and practical. Like Kirkpatrick before him, who had argued that Christians had to do more than secular temperance movements, Naughton put prayer first. He was especially disappointed that more did not turn out for the Special Day of Prayer appointed by the King in 1941: "Canada's great need at the moment is for spiritual awakening" he insisted.

At a victory loan rally at Richardson stadium in the same year, Dr Naughton discerned a "sinister influence in Kingston which seeks to prevent any public recognition of God in gatherings of this nature." Unfortunately, he did not elaborate. He seems to have been hinting at a sense of self-confidence that did not feel the need of God. He wondered whether Kingston was "the only place in the British Empire that had a public gathering on coronation day and did not pray for the king." Whatever we make of such royalist sentiments today, there is little doubt about the sincerity of Dr Naughton's Christian instincts.

When the war came to an end, bringing with it a semblance of stability, it seemed for a while that Dr Naughton's prayers for spiritual awakening were being answered.

A very special event was staged in 1945, preceding the main demobilization — a centenary celebration. The anniversary booklet declared that, having "weathered the storms of the first century of its existence, "St James' Church stands in a good state of physical repair, and its congregation looks to its Divine Master for spiritual fitness to carry on His work in the years to come."[23]

Boom years followed soon afterwards, not just an economic upturn but also years of confidence and growth for the church. Beneath this surface, however, other forces were at work, that would eventually show prophetic foresight in Dr Naughton's fears. But prospects were bright for the early post-war years, such that seeds of secularity being sown would not show through for some time.

PROFILE
DR NAUGHTON
RECTOR 1931-1953

John Douglas MacKenzie-Naughton was born in London, England, in 1886 and was raised there and in Arbroath, Scotland. He once went, as a teenage lark, to a Glasgow revival meeting. It changed his life. He said he felt as though he had been struck by lightning and from that moment determined to follow God's call — such he believed it to be — wherever it took him. With virtually no formal qualifications, a London missionary society sent him to Canada in 1906. He enrolled at Jarvis Collegiate and took five years of high school in two semesters.

Moving to the University of Toronto, he graduated with a first class honours degree in Oriental Languages in 1912, and an MA in 1913. In 1915 he married Eva May Burton (1887–1980), and they had two daughters, born after the war, Mary (now Peckover) and Margaret (now "Margot" McCurdy). He continued to study at Wycliffe College, obtaining another first class degree, this time his bachelor of divinity, specializing in Old Testament, in 1916. He was successively curate and vicar in three congregations in New Westminster, Vancouver and Victoria, BC.

Naughton enlisted for service in France during World War I, but actually went overseas with the Siberian Expeditionary Force — 1918–1919 — into which he was transferred. During his

John David MacKenzie-Naughton, a.k.a. "Dr Naughton," St James' fifth rector (shown here c. 1950).

This 1940s view of the rectory shows a day-room above the back door and a small second floor deck at the front (Dr. Naughton).

time in Vladivostock his observations led him to conclude that ". . . as a moral and spiritual force the Russian Church was dead." He himself found "a ray of sunshine" there in a Christian Japanese home from which a thriving Sunday School was conducted. "This is the true missionary spirit," he decided. "Here are these people away from their homeland, in the midst of a city where vice is rampant, letting their light shine for Christ and winning others to his service."[24]

Naughton returned to study and in 1924 he completed his doctor of divinity degree in systematic theology and New Testament, being only about the third Canadian ever to do this by course work. He wrote the PhD exams for seven hours solid, fed with coffee and sandwiches, because no one told him he could have had several days to complete! He must have been a registered post secondary student for about 16 years!

Dr Naughton came to Kingston in 1931, following Thomas Savery's return to Halifax the previous year. He announced his position in the text of his first sermon: "Other foundation can no man lay than that is laid, which is Jesus Christ."[25] In his gentle, formal way, he did a lot for the church. He preached with tremendous care, bringing his learning into the pulpit. He fostered the Queen's connection in several ways. And in Kingston he sat on the Executive and Investment Committees of the Diocesan Synod as well as being President of the Ministerial Association, an interdenominational group.

Dr Naughton never lost his military interest. While he was rector of St John's "Stone" Church, Saint John, New Brunswick he was chaplain to the Third Medium Brigade, New Brunswick Artillery, and during the war years in Kingston, to the Princess of Wales Own Regiment.[26] In Kingston he had the rank of Major.

He was very much the scholar and the soldier. This is confirmed by memories of those who knew him. He was well-liked in the officers' mess, and probably felt more at home there than in other contexts. As a shy person he certainly found domestic visits rather difficult. He once called at a parishioner's home during her daughter's birthday party, and assumed the serious discussion could continue regardless![27] But he was a faithful visitor nonetheless, calling on every parish household once a year. Family legend has it that in his first winter in Kingston, when he did not know his way around, this task entailed carrying a shovel to scrape snow off the sidewalk, where the street names were at that time inscribed![28]

When Dr Naughton did eventually get a car, he remembered its licence plate, as all other numbers, by a corresponding hymn number. He came home chuckling one year to ask his daughters "What do you suppose our licence number is this year? It's 'On our way rejoicing'!"

No one is gifted in every way, and what he might have felt he lacked in pastoral ministry was more than complemented by Eva Naughton. She started the fireside group for women left alone by their partners during the war, and was also deeply involved in many aspects of parish life, especially the Women's Auxiliary. She was on the national executive for a time. When Naomi Hunt came as the new rector's wife in 1953, she wondered how she could ever match the shining reputation of Eva Naughton for warm pastoral care.[29]

Dr Naughton was ever the quiet, thoughtful and somewhat reserved man. He struggled with the profound disturbing issues of the day, especially with how to square the atrocities of war with the providence of God. He also allowed his scholarly strength to be used to great advantage in encouraging an intellectual engagement with the gospel on the Queen's campus.

When eventually he left St James' it was to take up a position as professor at Wycliffe College, in 1953. Some parishioners thought that he would have been happy with such a chance long before.[30] The legacy he left at St James' was one that would prove valuable in years to come. He maintained and strengthened the evangelical tradition at St James', showing that it was quite compatible with a serious, even scholarly approach to the issues of the day.

7

The Golden Years

One holy church, one army strong
one steadfast, high intent;
one working band, one harvest-song,
one King omnipotent.

— Samuel Johnson[1]

A turkey dinner at St James' was announced in December 1946, to celebrate the return of war veterans. As befit the occasion, it was a festive affair, with entertainment from a string ensemble as well as fine food. It was also a symbolic meal, a signal of return to normality after the ravages of war. Doubtless, some tears were quietly shed for some who would never thus be welcomed home. But the dominant mood was determination to pick up the pieces and start afresh.

Familiar events continued to mark the weekly life of the church year. Sunday services, the Sunday School, Young People's Group, the WA and the choir flourished. A sacred choral meditation occurred each Good Friday, sometimes being quite ambitious. Bach's St Luke's Passion had been the music for 1944, for instance. In the summers of the late 1940s St James' joined with St Paul's for their services. A church vacation school was held for two weeks. Services were sometimes broadcast from St James' on CKWS. And the nurses from down the road came alternate years to St James' or to Chalmers for their graduation service.

It does seem, however, that Dr Naughton caught the scent of a shift in the wind direction as the new post-war era began. He redoubled his efforts to meet the challenges of the day. He sensed a subtle public indifference to the gospel,

Aerial photo of Stuartville,
1948. The Court House is on
the right, and St. Mary's
Cathedral in the far background (Wallace Berry).

Aerial photo of St James', 1948. The Court House is in the foreground (George Lilley, by permission).

Aerial photo of Queen's campus and St James', 1948 (George Lilley, by permission).

and tried to counter it with calls for renewal and attention to contemporary relevance. For example, popular preoccupation with fears of the hydrogen bomb presented opportunities. Though "scientists are working on the hydrogen bomb . . . that might obliterate the whole world," some things cannot be destroyed, he urged, quoting 2 Corinthians 5:1.

While Naughton had heavenly realities in mind as "indestructible," he also held on to the hope that the Dominion would yet be "God's Dominion." Post-war reconstruction could continue past patterns, it seemed. For some time he promoted the work of the "Anglican Advance" as representing the way forward. This movement could deepen the spiritual life of all if "each one realizes his or her personal relationship to the Lord Jesus Christ," he insisted.

So, after the austerity and restraint of the war years came the relief, the demobilization and then the consumer boom of the 1950s and 1960s. Reunited families settled back in their homes, bought cars and refrigerators and had children. During these years, the church was still the social hub of the neighbourhood, and people filled the pews every Sunday. Dr Naughton completed his steady, scholarly ministry at St James' to be replaced in 1953 by an energetic live-wire, Desmond Hunt. He, with his wife, Naomi, were to lead the church through its own boom years.

Considerable renewal did take place at St James' but two points must be noted. First, it came less through a specific movement like

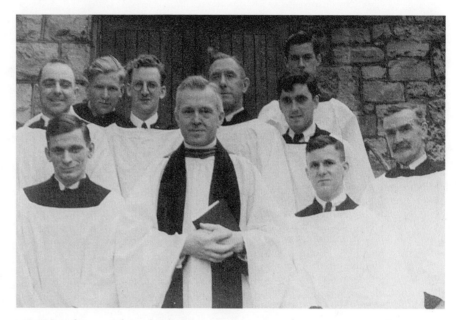

Dr Naughton with male choir members.

"New" snow removal
machines outside the rectory,
c. 1950 (Dr Naughton).

"Anglican Advance," more through a post-war mood and the arrival of a man of the moment. Second, the real gains and enthusiastic confidence of those years did not obliterate, but only obscured, the trends towards "indifference" that worried Dr Naughton.

POST-WAR BOOMS

During the Depression, through the war and into the 1950s the congregation had continued to live near the church building. Various records[2] show that many parishioners lived on adjacent streets such as Barrie, Division, George and Bagot, while others lived a few minutes walk away on University, Earl, Collingwood, Beverly, Queen's Crescent, Alfred, Frontenac, Victoria and Johnson. A few people lived on Queen or King Streets. The era of the motor car, and of commuting, had hardly begun. St James' was still a "parish church" in the old geographical sense. The people who attended St James' were very local and knew each other as neighbours.

Economically, Kingston's base was altering rapidly. The older locomotive works and ship-building companies, that had prospered so much during the war, began to falter. But new opportunities grew at Alcan and Du Pont, whose establishment largely accounted for the 34-percent growth of Kingston's population 1941–1951, from 36,772 to 49,246.[3] Situated in Kingston Township to the west of the city, these new industries began to pull the population further in that direction.

The fact that St James' was one of several older churches that were still downtown, and the increasing mobility that would be afforded by car-use would eventually produce a mix of local people and commuters at St James'.

The post-war baby boom, plus a large number of deaths among senior members of the congregation meant that the church became younger. This probably helps to account for some of the energy level during the 1950s, and for the number of church-related activities that St James' could support. But it also helps explain why alternatives to church also became more attractive. By the later fifties, while people might still attend Sunday morning, Ed Sullivan started to claim some Canadians from evening congregations.

When Desmond and Naomi Hunt arrived in Kingston in 1953 they were struck by what seemed like a stiff and starchy church. People dressed correctly and dispersed without talking together after the Sunday morning service. Yet they saw the place as having a great past and great potential. They set about to stimulate and support what would become one of the most lively churches in Kingston.

Around the hub of the church numerous activities revolved, several of which reflected the average age of the congregation. "What is your need? What are you interested in?" asked a flyer in 1963. The following options were available, as they had been for several years: For men, to be members of executive council, sidesmen, Sunday School teachers. Monthly men's meetings offered

The fishpond at the St James' garden party, June 13, 1956 (*Whig-Standard*).

Jean Thompson, of St James', holds an honour certificate at the Junior Auxiliary Rally, April 7, 1959 (*Whig-Standard*).

a dinner with speaker. Opportunities existed for joining "work parties" for the church. For women, the Women's church year, with a chance for responsibility, leadership, service, along with a monthly meeting. WA for missionary interest, fireside group for fellowship and service. Prayer and Bible study groups.

The list went on. For young people, "fortnightly gatherings of teenagers on Saturday nights for recreation and discussion of problems," all-age Sunday morning study classes, prayer and Bible study for "business people and older young people," Scouts, Rovers, Girl Guides, and for younger children, Brownies, Cubs, Junior WA ("with a view to missionary vision and training"), Sunday School, Nursery for children up to four on Sunday at 11.00. For families, "Opportunities . . . to get together for experiments in family living — family nights at the church."

The 1950s and early 1960s were also the golden years of the church choir. The choir not only led the congregation in musical worship, but represented St James' in the annual choral music festival. Run by the Rotarians, the festival competition was won by St James' several years in succession, from 1957–1963. The junior choir also won prizes for their efforts at this time.[4] A choral tradition of excellence was thus established that continued until the 1980s. Under Bill Barnes the choir would often compete in the Royal College of Organists' festival.

Lastly, this period saw another burst of building and renovation at St James'. New and renewed furniture and a new organ came in the late 1950s. A lighter freshness came to the interior of the building as old dark pews had the stain removed. New prayer desks and other items appeared, most given in memory of loved ones. On an ironic note, a credence table was among these. After the stern refusal of the nineteenth century congregation to include anything tainted by Rome, no murmur of objection was to be found. Credence tables had evidently lost their negative symbolic charge.

A special service of thanksgiving and dedication for the new effects occurred on February 25 1960.[5] The joyful assurance of these years is caught in the service. They sang "Glorious things of thee are spoken," "Angel voices ever singing," "City of God," and "Now thank we all our God." The choir sang Bach's anthem "In confidence and trust" and for the offertory, his "Now let faith's triumphant chorus." Nothing half-hearted or timid about this!

In the later sixties the facilities were expanded once more with a building programme that yielded some much-needed new space. Seen primarily as an addition to the Sunday School hall, the new rooms were for nursery, classrooms, washrooms and the new chapel. The Rogers Memorial Chapel had the old screens taken down to become the Rogers Room. It was also during this time (1964) that the Queen's steam heating system was extended to include St James' as well as the new biology hall. The building boom that brought utilitarian architecture to Kingston had

| After a service, early 1960s (Wallace Berry).

its milder counterpart in the concrete blocks of St James' new extension. The reason it was needed here, however, was that the church was still in a phase of assured growth. The work was completed in 1967.

Where, one might ask, did the financial support for building and outreach come from? The fact is that these were also the "golden years" of giving. After a half century of steady, modest giving, the rate per communicant increased markedly from 1950, rising steeply to a peak in 1965 (see Appendix I). The commitment to mission and to growth clearly inspired greater personal sacrifices.

When new lighting was installed in the church building, everyone held their breath until they knew what the Comer sisters would think. The pair of them were devoted to the church — as long, it seems, as nothing altered in the building! This time they demonstrated their disapproval by coming into the service in sunglasses. They got used to the new look before long!

LEADERSHIP AND LAITY

Although lay leaders had always played a significant part in St James', this tendency was reinforced during the 1950s and 1960s. Not only were there assistants — Raymond Carder and A. C. "Mac" McCullum — during the Hunt years, many others were encouraged to make their particular contribution to the overall life of the church.

Irene Cleland, who came to serious Christian commitment in that period, became the first woman representative from St James' at synod. She later admitted that Desmond Hunt had a gift for "making you *want* to do something."[6] Once in synod, she in turn spoke strongly in favour of encouraging the growth of women's Bible study groups in Kingston churches.

The Hunts were very good role models. Husband and wife led as a team, showing how people could work together. They even used a system of discreet signals, especially after church services on Sunday, to ensure that no visitor could escape without a welcome, if not an invitation for lunch or an introduction to a like-minded regular.

Those who assisted Hunt directly were given a fair amount of freedom to develop their own gifts. Indeed, Hunt attracted a variety of people who wanted to serve a kind of apprenticeship at St James'. The best known is Erasmus Bitarabeho, who came from Uganda in January 1964. He came, along with a compatriot, Shem Karorero, to gain pastoral experience and to further his education. Although he had graduated from seminary and had just been ordained deacon at Mbarara Cathedral, he had to take courses at KCVI before eventually going on to Wycliffe College.

It could be said, then, that the Hunts' ministry was very much bound up with enabling *others* to serve the church in one way or another, at St James' or in other parts of Canada and the world. They communicated their commitment and enthusiasm to one and all, leading by personal and joint example.

MISSIONS AND MARCHES

Desmond Hunt's watchword was "mission." While not for a moment neglecting pastoral matters, he clearly saw the health of the church in terms of its ability to look outward. He encouraged an "extended family" atmosphere in the church. He insisted that all should be serious about their Christian knowledge and growth; the Wednesday evening Bible meeting was an all-church event. But he also had an eye for opportunity. He grasped every chance, every medium, for living and for displaying the good news.

It comes as no surprise to learn, then, that Kingston Santa Claus parades included a truck bearing a full robed choir from St James'. Other initiatives bear the same stamp. Hunt appeared on a weekly phone-in radio show on CKWS, "Would you believe it?" St James' could on occasion be seen with other churches, processing through the streets on "marches of witness." Such innovative activities were an attempt to keep up with current trends, and to use whatever appropriate means available to connect the gospel with the world of the post-war consumer and baby boom.

Another new initiative was to hold missions. While Dr Naughton had been involved in several, it was in the Hunt years that the large-scale

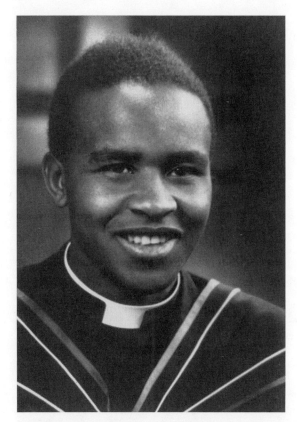

Erasmus Bitarabeho, at St James' from Uganda, 1964.

Mission team 1964. From back left, Lyndon Ruse, Desmond Hunt, Dick Rees, Ann Keenleyside, Rev. C. McCullum. Front row, Ron Steer, Jim McCullum.

Jim Slater and family, 1968.

Sunday evening "sing-song" during the Rees mission, 1964.

evangelistic mission came into its own. Often held in conjunction with other churches, Hunt invited prominent preachers — including the British Dick Lucas and Dick Rees — for several days of intensive mission in Kingston. St James' was also directly involved in the Leighton Ford mission —"Kingston for the King of Kings" — in 1964.[7] Hunt believed it was very important for Anglican churches to demonstrate their commitment to the gospel in a very public way.

Children's missions also featured within the activities of St James'. Speakers were invited, often during Holy Week, to address children. Tony Capon was one such speaker, and 50–75 youngsters would turn out to hear him. At one of these missions, Pamela Hunt, the rector's daughter, reported to Elizabeth Capon that she had accepted Christ as Saviour.[8]

Outreach was not limited to evangelistic activity, either. Support for Erasmus Bitarabeho was raised within the congregation, which also provided for him a family with which to lodge.[9] Somewhat in the background, social concern and involvement also continued during these years. In 1969, for instance, five church members attended a six week seminar on local community poverty, youth and corrections.[10]

| The building in good shape, 1964.

WORKING WITH OTHER CHURCHES

St James' has almost always enjoyed a close relation with other churches in Kingston, and not only Anglican ones. But the 1950s were boom years in this respect. Practical cooperation on several fronts was the order of the day. Of course, it would be artificial and misleading to disconnect Desmond Hunt from this, but others in the St James' congregation were also glad for the broadened network.

Inter-church missions were one way in which the cooperation was manifest. There was also an Evangelical Alliance in Kingston, of which St James' was a member, and also a Ministerial Association. Needless to say, Hunt was a leading light in both. His experience with these groups would have helped qualify him to become president of the national Evangelical Fellowship of Canada, formed in 1964.

Much was achieved during these years to overcome the mutual suspicion between the evangelical movement and Anglicanism. Of course, residual suspicions remained, but Hunt was a credible advertisement for evangelical Anglicanism. His involvement in inter-church missions endeared him to Baptists, Methodists and Pentecostals alike. Ministers from these churches often were invited to speak at St James', and Hunt at theirs. But his loyal Anglicanism ensured that he was not simply seen as a rebel. He was archdeacon in the diocese from 1960–1969. His stance and actions demanded that he be taken seriously.

As far as the broader Anglican Church was concerned, however, the ground lost nationally at the turn of the century was not recovered. Its Canadian centre had moved from Kingston long since and decline seemed the order of the day. Uncertainties about the role of a post-Christendom church, theological division and the challenges of an increasingly affluent and individualistic urban-industrial society were troubling the church.

The response of some churches was to become more inward looking, to defend tradition and to remain ambiguous about whatever mission the church might have. The broader church landscape had also been altering since the United Church was formed in 1925 and the number of smaller religious communities — Jewish, Lutheran — began to grow.

In this context, the role of St James' was distinctive. It never pursued a path of isolated Anglicanism, continuing rather to identify with the broader Protestant consensus that had emerged during the nineteenth century. This resonated with the idea of Canada as "God's Dominion," and was expressed in seeing the Christian churches as the social conscience and moral guardians of the nation.

To this consensus it brought an Anglican flavour — from the old Tory paternalism evidenced in concern for the poor and loyalty to the Empire to the maintaining of liturgical forms — but the flavour was to enrich the whole, not to be an end in itself. During the golden years in partic-

Guide parade, St James', June 1959.

Desmond Hunt addresses a
young peoples' group in the
Rogers room c. 1959
(Wallace Berry).

Sunday School students making full use of
the McMorine Hall, early 1960s
(Wallace Berry).

ular, St James' added to that mix an emphasis on mission and outreach. Conversion, discipleship, ecumenism and leadership all were special features of St James' from the post-war years to the late sixties.

THE QUEEN'S CONNECTION

Like most other universities, Queen's expanded after the Second World War, although the main boom was not until the later 1960s. This expansion brought with it early breezes that later heralded more severe cultural weather patterns.

At mid-century Vice-Principal McNeil could still cheerfully claim that "Queen's is essentially Christian." Registration forms, on which students noted their denomination, disclosed the data. "Non-denominationalism" of the university notwithstanding, in 1950 the student make-up was 35% United Church, 30% Anglican, 14% Presbyterian, 13% Roman Catholic and the rest, Baptist, Jewish, Lutheran and Christian Scientist.[11] It was also a national university, with only 10% of students coming from Kingston.

St James', being right on campus, was a natural church for Anglican students to attend, although many came from other denominations as well. Throughout each term, the Hunts had regular Sunday evening meetings in the rectory for students. Some present day members of St James' remember those nights — crowded on the living room carpet — with not a little nostalgia and gratitude. Hunt would sit down with students, try to answer their questions, and discuss with them the implications of his sermons. For many, such evenings were turning points in their lives.

For Hunt, student work was vitally strategic. When council was discussing whether or not to buy Arthur Place, the house next to the rectory on Barrie Street, it was its role in student ministry they had in mind. "It was recognised in council's discussions," say the minutes, "that [student] work is truly St James' greatest opportunity and challenge in the missionary field and that all members of the parish must be convinced of this . . . ."[12] That some might be less than sure is hinted here, but there is no indication that Hunt's commitment to students was not widely shared within the congregation.

Queen's Christian Fellowship (QCF), the InterVarsity Group, certainly found a "natural" affinity with St James'. A letter dated 1961 from the then president of QCF, Joanne Park, sums up the sense of involvement of St James' in work on campus: "The church has been vital to the activities of the group and has contributed a great deal to its witness to Christ . . . We appreciate the availability of your facilities which have been used for many activities, and we would like to say a special 'thanks' to the ladies and the caretaker . . . Both the archdeacon Hunt's and Rev. Carter's [sic] help has been invaluable."[13]

By the later sixties, however, Hunt was sensing a change of mood. He noted that ". . . we have to work harder to interest students in the church. Contacts are the important thing. They

Sunday School class in the McMorine Hall basement, early 1960s (Wallace Berry).

St James' junior baseball team with
John Kirkpatrick (left) and
"Chuck" Montizambert, c. 1961.

do not turn up in the crowds that they used to."[14] Similarly, at the special student receptions held at St James', the numbers, while still good, were starting to decline from those of the 1950s. In September 1969, for instance, 65 attended the start of term buffet supper.

Of course, the "town-gown" connection was strained from time-to-time. Some regular parishioners doubted the wisdom of paying quite such a lot of attention to students. Students, after all, could also bring disturbing new practices and ideas into the church. It was during the Hunt years that time-honoured dress codes were challenged; some female students showed up without hats! No doubt the wearing of jeans and sweaters followed.

THE COMFORTABLE PEW

In 1965, rather than produce the usual devotion book for Lent, the Anglican Church of Canada asked journalist Pierre Berton to give an outsider's view of the church. His book, *The Comfortable Pew*,[15] was an instant success and an all-time Canadian best-seller. Berton's beef, as an ex-Anglican, was that the church had become complacent, uncritical, culturally retarded. He likened what he saw to a commercial television network — "an agency for the comfort of its congregations." "Unless, like its founder, it stirs up the people by making large numbers of them acutely uncomfortable, . . . " he concluded, its survival is in doubt.

One might think that such an indictment

Jean Boyd, parish worker, 1968–9.

would have had little impact on St James', given the healthy growth of the post-war boom. St James' simply did not fit Berton's pessimistic picture. But in fact parishioners thought Berton had worthwhile things to say. Like many churches,[16] St James' set up Wednesday night discussion groups devoted to thinking through the implications of Berton's critique. Some were bothered about people assuming the church was there merely to serve them. While St James' did not seem to contain much radical discontent, enough people were unhappy with the apparent gap between church and modern life to try and find the means of closing it again.

For its first hundred years St James' had been able to take for granted its social and cultural role. As Toronto sociologist S.D. Clark had put it in 1948, the Canadian churches "as an integral part of the . . . community served as one of the means of entering into social relationships."[17] Now that role was being questioned. How then should the church see itself and its mission in the latter twentieth century? *The Comfortable Pew* was a symptom of the new self-awareness of the churches which is still present today.

The joyful assurance of the post-war period would give way to post-sixties turbulence. The gains made at St James' in numbers, outreach, depth of faith and willingness to take risks were obvious. The question was, would the strength built up in the boom years be enough to carry the church through the stormy seas ahead? Or, put another way, would the golden years turn out to be a golden sunset?

PROFILE
DESMOND AND NAOMI HUNT
DESMOND HUNT, RECTOR 1953–1968

Desmond Charles Hunt was born in Toronto, of parents who had emigrated from Dublin during the Great War. He was to become one of the last representatives of the Irish evangelical Anglicanism that had flourished in the nineteenth century, and which was the heritage of St James' and of institutions like Wycliffe College.[17] But he also translated that background into the realities of the later twentieth century, helping to forge forms of faith that would eventually carry it to the eve of the twenty-first.

Desmond — or "Des" as he was known to many — attended the Church of the Messiah as a boy. He graduated BA from the University in 1939 and from Wycliffe College in theology in 1942. He married Naomi in 1944. He became a curate at All Saint's Toronto before being appointed rector in Trinity Church, Ste Foy, Quebec and then in Johnstown, New York. In 1953 he came to St James' Kingston.

As a young man he had concluded that there must be more to the Bible than his minister and Sunday School teachers taught because "nothing could have been that dull." In a 1971 interview he said that "I found later, that by coming to even the most familiar stories with a sense of expectancy and excitement, sparks began to fly. If I was determined to get the meat of it," he went on,

Desmond Hunt, rector 1953-1968.

"new truths leaped out at me. I got a fresh charge every time."[19]

Coming from a lively parish in New York state the Hunts found St James' rather staid and dull. They were surprised at what seemed to them as the formality of services and the "proper" behaviour expected of church leaders. Things relaxed somewhat during their time at St James', though they were careful not to try to alter church life too fast. That they opened the rectory to all comers and proposed the removal of the dark walnut stain in the church building is symptomatic of their approach.

In a strong sense, Hunt continued the traditions in which St James' had begun over a century before. As church historian Ian Rennie has commented, "While Desmond knew of all the faults and foibles of his background, and sought to distance himself from them, he also knew its great strengths and cherished and developed them. As with his ancestors he believed and loved and studied the Bible. He was supremely a thoughtful Bible preacher, an expositor of Scripture, with all the eloquence, humor and imagination for which the Irish are justly famous."[20]

It was with heavy hearts, but much gratitude that the congregation had to bid the Hunts farewell in 1969. Hunt returned to his boyhood church, Messiah, Toronto, as rector from which he conducted the famous "Tuesday on the Square" programme at Holy Trinity to which 200 business people came each week. Wycliffe College honoured him with a doctor of divinity degree in

The Hunt family in the rectory living room, c. 1958. From left, Rachel, Desmond, Pamela, Jonathan, Christopher, and Naomi.

1977 and in 1981 he was consecrated as a suffragan bishop in St Paul's, Bloor Street. He retired in 1986, but continued as an assistant at St Paul's and went on writing and leading parish missions.

When he died in July 1993, aged 75, over 1200 people whose lives had been touched through his work came for the funeral. Bishop Peter Mason noted that "He loved and cared deeply for the church . . . Desmond loved the God-givenness of the church's liturgy and music and thrived in his work with students at the Inter-Varsity Christian Fellowship, at Wycliffe College and with members of the Church Army and in his ecumenical ministry."

Naomi, very much his partner in ministry throughout, continues to live in Toronto. Pam, his daughter, continues to keep in touch with St James' from Manila, the Philippines, where she works at Faith Academy for the Overseas Missionary Fellowship. Hunt's own comment, made in 1981, sums up what his approach had been, at St James', as elsewhere: "To be where God wants you and to know it, is a strong point about parish ministry."[21] He believed in the importance of the local parish church, but also encouraged contact with others, of whatever church, engaged in the same mission in the modern world. That confident sense of calling sustained him in the task.

8

A Subtle Secularity

"I stop going to Sunday School."
— Margaret Atwood[1]

The "sixties" was a cultural sea-change throughout the Western world. The period of rapid and radical change actually lasted until about 1973. Despite the brief sense of national euphoria as Canada celebrated its century of confederation and first flew the maple leaf flag, turbulent conditions were all around. The oil crisis revealed a new world force to be reckoned with. Quebec separatism hit the headlines. Student revolt broke out in Europe, the USA, and even rippled into Queen's. But while in retrospect the changes seem profound, at the time they were contained, not cataclysmic.

The transformation involved the wholesale moving of social and cultural boundary markers that had been in place for decades, if not centuries. But in keeping with the marker-moving metaphor, it was a covert operation. Instead of deference to elders, the focus shifted to the young, now ready to spend new-found money on music and clothes. Whereas men had usually assumed "natural" leadership roles, women began more strenuously to challenge the status quo. And the churches, for long at the centre of social and family life, started lost out to alternative attractions at a quickening pace.

Of course, these cultural changes did not emerge overnight. Rather, some critical events in the sixties weakened the surface so much that underlying pressures broke through, eventually becoming visible to all. Immigration patterns had steadily eroded the old social bases of English and French Canada, introducing a variety of new religious practices. But it was not obvious until after the sixties that the old evangelical consensus was gone, especially in Ontario.

Hopes for "God's dominion" were battered by war and depression, and theologies often modified to be more inclusive, less evangelistic. And the post-war religious boom further obscured the underlying realities of change.

What was once taken-for-granted became questionable. Margaret Atwood's characters stopped going to Sunday School.[2] Pluralism eroded the securities of a single expression of religion. Above all, as far as St James' is concerned, new patterns of social life such as commuting and "working women" altered the dynamics of a church-in-a-neighbourhood. When combined with the futuristic pull of fast-growing new technologies of aero-space and electronics, any group that seemed to have ties with the past found the going hard. Along with horse-drawn carts and the family farm, the church appeared as a victim of social and cultural progress.

For a number of reasons, then, the Canadian slide into secularity was sudden. Time-honoured and taken-for-granted ties were cut between public life and the religion of the churches. Unlike the USA, where secularity has not eroded levels of churchgoing (secularity grows *within* American churches), in Canada it had the opposite effect. People evacuated the churches. Unlike Britain, where secularization was a much longer drawn-out process, it seemed swift and, eventually, savage, in Canada. Perhaps the very strength of church life and influence earlier in the century meant that secularity, when it came, would be more complete.[3] At St James', while

these changes were not dramatic, they became decisive. While the pews did not empty overnight, a subtle secularity was abroad.

THE SIXTIES AND AFTER AT ST JAMES'

St James' was buffeted by the waves of change as much as any church, though its position was peculiar. For one thing, the previous two decades really had been golden years in the parish. St James' was vitally involved in evangelistic outreach, developing a welcoming atmosphere in the church, student ministry and missionary work. It was also part of an interdenominational group of churches in the city that saw themselves as working together for the kingdom of God, and of a national church that had yet to recognise the scope of the changes then occurring. It has to be said, however, that little evidence of broader social concern exists for this time.

When the weather changed, St James', being on the edge of Queen's campus, had less shelter than some churches from the cultural winds blowing through Canada. While a rural or even a suburban parish might have enjoyed partial insulation from their full effect, a downtown church, near the business core and the university, did not. On the other hand, Kingston was not Toronto or Montreal. Both city and university were somewhat more conservative and traditional, and thus felt the force of changing conditions a little more gently.

At St James' there was an uneasy sense that

something was going on, but it was not clear what. The mood changed. Some people left after Hunt moved on. Others wanted things different. But defection and discouragement were only a sub-plot. Much momentum was maintained. St James' certainly did not lose completely its distinctive character in the late sixties and early seventies. But something was missing, or, rather, seemed to be slipping away.

With hindsight, things start to become clearer. Canada in general, and the city of Kingston in particular, were going through significant alterations, some of which were echoed in the church. Alongside the more obvious changes — the appearance of student radicalism, the shift towards service industries — were subtler ones that would have a great effect on the church.

One of the most significant was that women joined the paid labour force in ever-increasing numbers, as Kingston became more service-oriented. This posed a threat to one of the key factors that had for decades contributed profoundly to the ongoing life of the church. Women would become less available for daytime activities and involvement. So their role in fostering a sense of community was diluted. The church would be slow in recognising and coming to terms with this new reality.[4]

A second change was the new geography of church involvement. The local community ceased to be central to the life of St James' as students took over old Stuartville family homes and as greater mobility allowed people to travel in from afield. The jury is still out on how the church would respond to these changes; the impact of these social and cultural upheavals is still felt today.

Another feature of this period was ecumenism. Under the banner of "Christian unity" joint services were held and church members from different churches discussed the potential for increased contact and cooperation. Cynics might say that the churches attempted to cope with declining numbers through joining forces. Whether or not this was the case, it is possible that a subtle shift was taking place. The quest for unity no longer seemed to be for the sake of a common *mission* to the world. Rather, unity appears to have been sought as an end in itself.

KINGSTON AND ST JAMES' IN TRANSITION

Before the war, life in old Stuartville still had been oriented toward the downtown and the waterfront. After the war, the focus shifted somewhat, but not yet in ways that affected directly the St James' neighbourhood. However, the impact of industrial and suburban development in the Kingston and even Ernestown townships to the west skewed that focus in the sixties. As the old waterfront locomotive, coal and shipping industries declined and crumbled, the new initiatives grew and prospered. But the downtown residential area, Sydenham Ward, whose population had been draining in the sixties, started to fill again in the seventies.[5]

Queen's post-war boom put many more students into rented housing in Sydenham ward. Many homes once occupied by — some built by — St James' members were now let to students. Consequently, far fewer families lived near the church building. As the downtown area began to attract new kinds of tourism and service jobs, some older homes did receive a face-lift, and something of a renewed residential life began to develop. But the cost of downtown living affected who could afford homes which meant that the nature of families living nearby was very different from those of old Stuartville. In addition, apartment blocks appeared near the water, which were attractive to older and professional people.

Kingston as a site for tourism and service industries was encouraged by events such as Kingston's selection for the sailing Olympics in 1976 and the expansion of sub-capital administrative functions alluded to elsewhere. These trends, along with rising proportions of car ownership, also meant that residence and workplace could become increasingly remote. And if you travel for work, education and entertainment, why not for church as well? Fewer families lived in the immediate neighbourhood of St James'; more started to commute to church from further away. The shift away from a local to a scattered community was decisive. It would eventually alter people's understanding of what church was all about.

The growth of service industries, tourism, education, administration and commerce in Kingston also opened new opportunities for female employment. Although it would be hard to obtain the actual figures for St James', there is no reason to suppose that St James' was less affected than any other group by general trends. Women made up 18.5% of the Canadian labour force in 1941, 40.8% by 1981. The largest rise was from 27.3% in 1961 to 34.6% in 1971.[6] The circumstantial evidence that this affected St James' is strong. The WA, later Anglican Church Women, still so active in the 1950s and early 1960s, had all but collapsed by the later 1980s.

SEEKING STRATEGY

Against this backdrop, the implicit strategy adopted by the church was a careful holding operation. Emphases emerged that stressed the significance of internal parish life, tightened the ties with the diocese and explored the chances for church cooperation. Not that new initiatives were absent or that all existing ministries faltered. Rather, to cope with cultural confusion and incipient social instability, the mood of the church started to shift subtly from offensive to defensive action, from an assumption of strength to consciousness of weakness, from mission to maintenance.[7]

The difficulties experienced in the 1969 change of rectors is partly understandable in this light. For a start, the church had a hard time selecting a replacement for Desmond Hunt. These were eventually resolved in the discovery of a

Delegates from the Ontario Diocese attending the General Synod at Laval University, Quebec, in June 1975, including, left, "Bill" Barnes and second from right, Gordon Hendra.

young candidate in Winnipeg who, when telephoned by a churchwarden, agreed to come for an interview the very next day![8] Gordon and Allie Hendra arrived in Kingston to a warm welcome.

By any standards, the Hunts were hard to follow. The new rector knew well what the Hunts' ministry had been like. Wisely, Hendra did not try to be another Desmond Hunt. In any case, while he felt comfortable in an evangelical congregation, Hendra's churchmanship was considerably broader than Hunt's. Powerful preaching and energetic missionary zeal were not his metier, but he had a gift for getting alongside people and winning their confidence. Many were helped by his careful sermons. Student work continued, now with a quest for a chaplain,[9] and work with St James' own young people increased.

It cannot be said that these years at St James' were always plain sailing. Some felt that the church was changing direction as well as slowing down after the energetic evangelicalism of the previous decades. There was a feeling that St James' could be in danger of submerging its unique identity under a vague Anglicanism.

A parish planning exercise had begun, not long after Hendra arrived, to determine some direction for the church. This was most intense in 1971, when different subcommittees met with parishioners for open discussion. Areas represented were the chaplaincy, financial commitment and physical resources, community needs, parish needs, church education, worship, and church union. Various priorities were identified, although these did not exclude other initiatives.

One such initiative was a closer identification with the diocese. With its historic reputation as a somewhat idiosyncratic church within the diocese, St James' now allowed itself to be — partially! — domesticated. Not that St James' had enjoyed no diocesan representation. Far from it.[10] But there was a new sense that St James' should identify more with the diocese than with the group of evangelical churches of which it had previously been one.

With other Anglicans, St James' considered closer cooperation with the United Church. Already the 1971 "red hymnbook" represented some groundwork towards common worship. So people from St James' and from Chalmers went to each others' services and also organized a number of joint events. By 1975, however, the experiments faltered at a national level. The bishops judged union inappropriate and soon afterwards the national synod, meeting in Quebec City, voted against it.

The reaction to the "red hymnbook" was in some ways symptomatic of ecumenical miscalculation. While it seems that St James' people took to it without loud protest, other members of both Anglican and United Church congregations saw the book as a sell-out to the other. Each believed the resulting selection of hymns represented the dominant choices of the other!

Interdenominational cooperation was explored at other levels too. Roman Catholics preached at St James', probably for the first time.[11] And people from St James' met with others from First Baptist, Chalmers' and Sydenham Street United, and St Mark's Lutheran for Lent Sunday evening programmes. Arranged by a joint planning group, the event was like a Lent school, with different groups meeting to discuss a variety of themes. A hundred and more met each week, although participation plummeted when the study group format was replaced in the late 1970s by a devotional service. It evaporated soon afterwards.

Sunday activities changed, no doubt in response to the congregation's changing living and working arrangements. In the early days communion was at 9.00 a.m. Sunday, followed by Morning Prayer at 11.00 (except the first of the month which was communion). After evening prayer at 7.00 anything from 15–30 students met in the rectory to discuss issues of Christian faith, just as they had when the Hunts were there. Parishioners provided snacks. This lasted until the mid-1970s.

Attempts were made to try to involve the congregation more. The communion table was moved out from the wall so the celebrant could face the congregation, and 11.00 a.m. became a communion service. A coffee hour began after the 9.00 a.m. communion. Despite double choir quartets who sang motets *a capella*, evening prayer gradually lessened in attendance and was dropped in the mid 1970s.

Watch those clothes! Frank Mitchell often used to help out with packing the bales from the WA. One warm day he loosened, then removed his tie. Later in the day he realised, on looking round for the tie, that it must have been dispatched for the North-West Territories! On another occasion Bessie Comer folded her coat in the corner of the hall during a busy church bazaar. You guessed it! To her indignation she discovered her coat had been sold.

In 1975 a dozen or so "household fellowships" were started. They met every month in each others' homes for a simple meal. The idea was inspired by the "foyer" groups at Coventry Cathedral in England, and continued successfully for nearly two years. St James' had begun small groups before, and would see them again. After the sixties, such changes took place increasingly. With a more transient congregation and with a higher turnover, memories shortened and some experiments, though worthwhile, did not last long.

The most significant innovation — in that it has stood the test of time — was a Wednesday morning communion. The old 10.00 a.m. service on Wednesday had less than twenty attending, predominantly women who were at home in the daytime, and numbers were dwindling. Two members[12] proposed a "pre-work" communion during Lent. The idea caught on fast, and soon thirty to forty, mainly students, came each week in term. A coffee and muffins breakfast followed.

Students reported that "It's great, starting the day with Jesus!" Occasionally, communion would occur "in the round" with the elements being passed from one to the other, along with guitar-led folk singing.[13]

Young people were still in evidence; there was even a parish hockey team! 1969–70 was a record season for the "Mites" (7 and 8 year olds) hockey team that won no less than 15 games, tied 3 and lost one! St James' people were involved with others in starting a "Meals-on-Wheels" service to shut-ins, which formed the basis for the service — now not church-based — that still runs today. The guitar was introduced for the first time as an accompaniment for the junior choir.[14] And Queen's students continued to look on St James' as a "home away from home" and as a source of fellowship and counsel.[15]

STUDENT LIFE

The 1950s and 1960s had been decades of enormous growth at Queen's. Between 1961 and 1968 the student population almost doubled. Buildings sprang up all over the old campus, and a new campus was established for the Duncan McArthur College of Education. New departments such as film studies, computing science and sociology were launched. By the early seventies, Queen's had developed into a institution of nearly 10,000 students. Growth was actually slowed in order to ensure that the "spirit" of the school would not be lost.

Radicalism hit many campuses during the

late sixties and early seventies but as a student society vice-president said, "Queen's was the last to get it and the first to lose it."[16] The nearest thing to confrontation came in 1970 when Chuck Edwards, a chemical engineering student and member of the Free Socialist Movement, accused his thesis supervisor of forcing him to choose between studies and his political activities. The RCMP was on campus and a major enquiry ensued. The storm took a while to calm.

At about this time a "Social Action Group" from Queen's asked permission to use the McMorine Hall for their meetings. Imagine the consternation when parishioners on campus noticed posters advertising the meetings at St James' under the sign of a hammer and sickle! No wonder they had a hard time finding a campus room. Anyway, the "communists" came as agreed, despite some parish protest.

Some people noted another kind of mood emerging on campus during the growth period. Queen's, that had for decades offered a high quality post-secondary education at reasonable cost, now began to include a larger proportion of better off students among its ranks. One physics professor noted that the 1970s was a decade in which a more materialistic attitude seemed to pervade the student world. Notions of learning as a worthwhile endeavour in its own right started to lose out to the idea that it should be job-related.[17]

At the public level, relations with Queen's continued cordial and cooperative. At the time of the 1975 St James' anniversary a special Queen's service was held. But its temper was different from those that had taken place earlier in the century. It was more a celebration of good relations, less a moment for mission. Principal John Deutsch and Chancellor Roland Michener read lessons and the Queen's ensemble sang.

It seems that not only the Social Action Group was *persona non grata* on campus near this time. QCF also had trouble finding a meeting place so for a while it used the McMorine Hall. St James' also hosted a regular Thursday luncheon for faculty and staff to discuss questions of faith and modern life. But the most significant feature of the St James'-Queen's relation in the seventies was the development of the Anglican chaplaincy.

The early hopes of a chaplaincy were realized in 1974 when Eric Howes came to be assistant at St James' and Anglican chaplain at Queen's. The diocese agreed to a fifty-fifty cost split with St James'. Howes and his wife lived — with their pet rat — at Arthur Place, 148 Barrie Street. In 1976 Douglass Ray, along with his wife Sandy, took over from the Howes. When Arthur Place was sold they lived on Earl Street. Events took place at the chaplain's apartment, including a weekly student Bible study and an informal eucharist. As well, a Wednesday morning communion continued in the St James' chancel. But the main chaplaincy venue was the Grey House on Queen's Crescent.

Activities were geared mainly to meeting the

needs of Anglican students on campus, and to an ecumenical programme known as LARC (Lutheran, Anglican, Roman Catholic). Potluck suppers, with speaker, were a regular feature, as were retreats held with the other chaplaincy groups. Hikes, canoe trips and other sports events completed the picture. The scale seems to have been fairly small. While 33 student names and addresses are listed in September 1974, for instance, it appears from the evaluation of chaplaincy work that only a dozen or so students actually came to a typical event.

To complete the story of the chaplaincy, reference must be made to Arthur Place. Though the chaplaincy work continued under the aegis of St James' until after Douglass Ray left in 1978, it was clear that eventually another site would have to be found if Arthur Place was not the meeting place. The major controversy of the seventies was whether or not to sell this valuable property in order to rid the church of a millstone of debt. Dark threats about resignation were muttered and some feared a major debacle.

The eventual church meeting was the most heated many could remember. In the end Arthur Place slipped out of St James' hands, to the relief of those who had been trying in vain to balance the books ever since the building of the Sunday School rooms in the mid-sixties. One former warden was to leave the church following this. No one foresaw the tower crisis of the 1990s,

when some were to regret the lack of collateral that Arthur Place would have afforded.

THE SEVENTIES IN PERSPECTIVE

The seventies are not looked back on with anything like the affectionate feelings generated by the experience of the fifties and sixties. Yet one suspects that the reasons for this have as much to do with what was happening *to* the church as what was happening *in* the church. The St James' congregation aged somewhat, and more women found their way into paid employment. Stronger links were forged with the diocese. At the same time, forward-looking policies were adopted, like attempting to balance the lay leadership between Queen's people and others.

The seventies was a decade of — largely-failed — ecumenism. The hoped-for closer connections between St James' and Chalmers' fizzled out and each church chose to go her own way. Despite this formal independence, however, mutual understanding had been enhanced. On campus, ecumenical activities drew students together from different traditions, but no permanent united witness resulted.

Yet ecumenical experiments did have some long-term effects. For instance, the Kingston Ministerial Association had been decidedly Protestant until the sixties. Max Putnam, of St Andrew's Presbyterian Church, had argued that

Roman Catholics should be included. But the argument was won in the seventies when Catholic lay-people attended charismatic meetings, such as those at the Gospel Tabernacle (then on MacDonnell Street).

Curiously enough, the decisive General Synod meeting in 1975 that rejected church union, also opened the way for women to be ordained in the Anglican church. The fruits of this were to be realised at St James' within the next few years. But the same movement towards the feminizing of the professions also took many women *out* of the kind of active, voluntary involvement on which St James', like the other churches, had relied for many decades. Both trends were significant. But the first was as public and well-known as the second was hidden and unrecognised.

After the seventies, even more serious attention had to be paid to the question of what the church stood for. The ebullient sixties were well past. The holding operation of the seventies in many ways succeeded, but could not be maintained indefinitely. Old assumptions about the monolithic errors of Rome or the time-honoured fixity of gender roles were now in serious doubt. St James' was gathering strength for a renewed burst of experiment, risk, and change.

PROFILE
GORDON HENDRA
RECTOR 1969-1978

Gordon Hendra was born in Toronto on April 7, 1928, the son of an independent grocer. His family were members of St Paul's, Bloor Street. He attended Jarvis Collegiate, followed by Victoria College, University of Toronto and subsequently — what seemed to be the "natural" choice — Wycliffe College, from which he graduated B.D. in 1953. He married Allie Black, and their family eventually included four children, Catherine, Carol, John and Peter.

Hendra's ministry began as a curate with St Timothy's Toronto after he received his L.Th. in 1952. They moved west in 1954, first to Rimbey-Sylvan Lake-Eckville in Calgary diocese, and then Hendra became successively rector of St Marks', Calgary, 1957-1965 and Holy Trinity, Winnipeg 1965-1969. The latter was a lively, downtown church, rather larger than St James'.

Hendra knew all about Desmond Hunt's ministry when he arrived, and was delighted to find such an active congregation at St James'. It was busy, and the students' involvement kept church leaders on their toes! Hendra tried to innovate, where appropriate, but he also believed in organizational links. He fostered the relationship between St James' and the diocese, and he argued that church leadership should not be comprised solely of Queen's personnel. A town-gown, church-diocese equipoise was what he sought.

In 1978 Hendra, who had been a cathedral canon in Winnipeg, was asked to be programme director and executive assistant to the bishop. After some hesitation, he accepted, and later became archdeacon of Kingston, in 1983. From 1988-1990 he was executive archdeacon for the diocese, but returned to a final spell of parish life at St Mark's, Barriefield 1991-1994. He retired on December 31, 1994.

In September 1970 St James' celebrated its 125th anniversary with a dinner and a thanksgiving service. Included at the dinner were Queen's principal John Deutsch, mayor Valerie Swain and MLA Syl Apps. Allan Anderson, the diocesan archivist, gave a talk on St James' history. For the service, the retired bishop of Calgary, George R. Calvert, had returned to his home church as guest preacher. His sermon corrected some misconceptions about faith: ". . . it is too often thought of as something you have or haven't got. We have a queer idea that it is a kind of aroma that enshrouds certain people. Nonsense. Faith is always a dynamic power. It is full of push. It is full of confidence. It is a matter of the assurance of the presence of the Lord . . . As you look back and think of the steadfastness of those who went before us, faith really means something."[18]

Gordon Hendra,
rector 1969–1978.

9

Finding New Ways Forward

Then he took his contradictions out
And he splashed them on my brow
So which words was I then to doubt
When choosing what to vow
Should I choose them all — should I make them mine
The sermons, the hymns and the valentines
And he asked for truth and he asked for time
And he asked for only now

— Joni Mitchell[1]

Whatever way you look at it, St James', like other churches, had to find new ways forward after the sixties. The congregation was ageing; few younger people were coming to take their place. Numbers were steadily falling (see Appendix I). Financially, churches were starting to feel the post-boom squeeze and giving was going down. Perhaps most significant, the church could no longer take for granted its place on the social and cultural scene. On the margin of a large university campus, St James' felt these forces acutely.

The cultural shifts commonly referred to as the "sixties" actually happened from the mid-sixties to the mid-seventies. So while at St James' Gordon Hendra oversaw the transition, it was Bob and Mollie Brow — who came in 1978 — who were faced with the full force of the post-sixties phenomenon. In several respects, however, their coming was a Godsend. They came with eyes already open to cultural difference, having spent much of their lives in India. And they were prepared to experiment, partly because they thought creatively about the mission of the church, but also because they could see the writing on the wall for the church if they did not.

EXPERIMENTS WITH CHANGE

When the warden, Paul Speight, contacted the Brows with the possibility of their coming to St James' their first question was this; "Will the ministry at St James' be a challenge? We don't want a sinecure," they went on, "We're not interested in a rich, placid church without a challenge."[2]

They discovered early on that St James' was indeed no sinecure. Young people were sparse and there were no babies. Brow found himself burying many and baptising very few. The streets around the building no longer bustled with the daily round of shopping, children playing, old men talking on the corner. Victorian frame and brick houses, torn down to make way for a temporary structure, were eventually replaced with a looming new technology building across Union Street.[3] The challenge for the Brows was to check for signs of life and focus first aid attention on those areas.

At Little Trinity, Toronto, working with Harry Robinson, the Brows had been developing

| Bob and Mollie Brow.

their ideas on the church as a sort of school. Baptism was like enrollment, and from there the task was to learn to know God and to love each other. At St James' they wanted to be able to "welcome atheists, doubters and those who wonder whether life has any meaning at all." For, Brow insisted, "it is only working through the challenges they bring, can we grow and learn and strengthen our own faith."[4] Although some parishioners said they only accepted this "kicking and dragging their feet," most were grateful for the experience!

The Brows questioned the *status quo*, disturbed the comfortable and challenged the complacent. Like Robert Rogers in the mid-nineteenth century, they were unafraid to place scripture above tradition. What bothered some, however, was that they would also raise queries about how far received doctrine was really what the Bible taught. For them, certainty had more to do with being sure of God's love than being precise on some more "disputable" doctrinal points. Without doubt, they made people think about their faith.

Not for the first time in the history of St James', the emphasis on being informed and involved Christians led someone into a change of direction, towards ordained ministry. David Ward was a professor in the Queen's chemistry department. He and his wife came to St James' when the Brows had been there just one year. He became first a lay leader at St James', undertook theological studies, and then became an assistant to Bob Brow.

Other younger people made their way to St James', and soon after, guitars began to feature in a new Sunday evening service. The more contemporary music and the freedom that came with it attracted others, and soon a hundred and more were crammed into the Rogers' Room for these Sunday evening meetings. The choir also swelled under Bill Barnes' leadership and with the influx of some from the "evening" worshippers. Later on the guitar would be introduced into the 10.30 Sunday service, generally during communion. Different worship forms did not experience an entirely smooth ride, however. The Sunday evening meeting, for instance, was by no means a permanent fixture.

The Book of Alternative Services appeared in 1985. But even before it was launched Bob Brow used sections from it on duplicated service sheets. The reaction was seismic. The change seemed too revolutionary, too rapid, or just plain unnecessary to some people. Why, "we have *always* used the little old maroon prayer book!" Controversy over the new "green book" continued for some time, to Brow's chagrin. Indeed, it continues to this day. Some prefer the beauty of the traditional prose, others the theology of the *Book of Common Prayer*. For others, of course, *any* change is gratuitous, even though the authors of the *Book of Common Prayer* never intended their forms to be fixed forever.

Another innovation that was better received — though it too faltered after several years — came with a new couple who joined St James' from Montreal. Faith and Earle Thomas suggested that an Order of St Luke chapter be started. Brow agreed to take the training course to become chaplain. Thus began a serious healing ministry with a team of a dozen. One month was especially memorable. Two women diagnosed with different terminal conditions were prayed for and are still alive today. And when a little boy severed his spinal cord falling down a set of stairs his parents were told he would be a blind, deaf, mute with no feeling. The healing team prayed, persistently, and today he is a lively ten year old.

The other assistant in these years was Marie Warner, the first ordained woman to have a formal role at St James'. This was significant, because it signalled a willingness to take seriously new questions of women's consciousness and role within the church. Bob Brow would not have described himself as a feminist when he came to St James' in 1978. But he made much effort to see things through women's eyes, and to be as inclusive as possible. He and Marie Warner showed that you do not have to agree on every detail in order to work together.

The news spread that St James' was a church where women could feel at home. Several women met together to talk over issues of how men and women relate in church. In 1980 Irene Cleland was appointed as the first female warden. One Queen's student, Ann Jervis, who led the young people's work 1977–78, went on to study theology. Now a professor at Wycliffe College, she is a spokesperson for biblical concern on gender issues.

From 1975 to 1993 Bill Barnes, a professor in the Queen's English department, was organist and music director at St James'. He encouraged Queen's people to join the choir, for which he often composed music. And he was delighted to find an occasional student for whom the biblical background of certain poems did not have to be explained, laboriously. He tied in his spiritual journey with the material he taught, making it "very rich, very real." [5]

Despite diabetes, dialysis, lameness and the loss of one leg at the knee, then the other, and sporadic blindness, he taught, wrote, composed and lived with remarkable courage. No plaster saint, however, the one with a thorn in the flesh could also be such to others. Stubbornness in the face of suffering spilled over into other areas. He often disturbed the faithful with his earthiness and his unorthodox lifestyle, and he could clash with the local powers-that-be.

OUTLOOK AND OUTREACH

During 1979, the first year of the Brows' time at St James', a "Parish Purpose" statement was developed. Modelled closely on the New Testament description of the church in the Book of Acts, it began with Christ's commission to "make disciples of all nations." From this two purposes flowed; "to persuade people in the area of Kingston to become learners (disciples) and to impart to them all that Jesus commanded us" and "to support the missionary work of the Christian church throughout the world . . . ."

Specifically, the Acts text produced four focus areas: teaching, fellowship, breaking of bread and prayer. Each heading was then amplified, so that fellowship, for instance, included everything from coffee hours to sharing with Christians from other churches and "throughout the world." This area, fellowship, certainly expanded in the 1980s.

During this time St James' grew gradually into a community, or, better, a loose network of small groups. From these groups, the church spread its influence in new and creative ways. Irene Cleland said of these years, "the most exciting aspect of Robert Brow's ministry has been his encouragement of groups. Groups that meet for Bible study, prayer, music, theatre and to share meals. These groups have provided the parish and the community with a chance to learn and celebrate the learning together."[6]

Events initiated in the earlier 1970s continued into the 1980s. The most important were the Wednesday communion and breakfast and the Thursday potluck. In place of the older, taken-for-granted events that once gathered churchpeople together, special ones like these had to be invented to pull together the now scattering, busy congregation. The trick was to find something that would be both attractive to a broad range of people and would not take too big a toll of diary space.

For a number of years, the Thursday evening family potluck was a regular event in the weekly calendar. The idea was that the church could get together for a meal before various activities that took place in the later evening; choir, Anglican Church Women (ACW) and so on. After a while, the potluck, which was preceded by communion, became known as a place of welcome for all.

A newcomer once introduced himself as he sat down to eat, and was greeted with "Hi! Glad to meet you. I am Charles, and I'm a homosexual, this is Adrian, who's manic depressive, and this is Gerald, who's a schizophrenic."[7] While this was exactly in line with what the Brows and others saw as part of church ministry, some saw it differently. Combining family supper with what some saw as a soup kitchen could not work, the dissenters thought. By 1989, the group was down to a handful, and the supper was organized single-handedly by Marie Warner. Several mourned its loss for some time to come.

An eighties' initiative was the mothers' group, which spun off a women's prayer group. Within a short time thirty and forty mothers were meeting weekly, led by Sue Caldwell and Susie Rogerson. They discussed issues relating to parenting, but also the challenges of belief and Christian living in an increasingly secular society. Student babysitters were engaged to free their parents for this hour. Without the local neighbourhood of times past, role-models and opportunities to share at a basic level are few and far between. The mothers' group met a real need, in a practical way.

Equally, an older era of missionary expansion was at a close. The throb had dulled in the civilizing impulse that had once helped galvanize the WA into sending bales to faraway places and young people into volunteering for service overseas. Canada now was a multi-cultural country, trying to distinguish itself from the American melting pot by asserting that the mutual respect of the mosaic was a better way. While the church still supported medical and teaching missionary outreach, another opportunity to express Christian love within the chastened, decolonised mode came when Vietnamese "boatpeople" started arriving as refugees.

Thus in 1980 St James', like several other churches, mounted a project to support six young Vietnamese men in their early twenties. The arrangements were made through World Vision, the approval of the bishop and the Department of Immigration was obtained, and the church raised over $4,000, with promises of $300 per month. Housing was found near Sir John A. and Counter Street, and a number of households and individuals oversaw the process of finding initial supplies and goods to set up home. Elaine Brunke became their Canadian mother, teaching them local customs and etiquette. Efforts were made to understand Vietnamese culture and a few words of language, and for many months the church was made very directly aware of situations very different from those in Kingston.

During the eighties deliberate attempts were made to balance, combine, or, better, to integrate different aspects of outreach. The Brows tried hard to be accessible, and to make clear that they knew people no longer came to church because of social custom. Hence the meetings arranged, not only with students in mind, for "atheists, doubters and fence sitters." The first of these, entitled "Who is God, and where on earth is he, or she?" raised a few eyebrows. Brow did not regard the pulpit as somewhere he could be "two metres above contradiction" or the sermon as an authoritative communiqué that was beyond discussion. While this did not endear him to those for whom theological correctness was paramount, it did create a sense of the openness of church to varying currents of opinion.

The sense of open possibilities, of experiment and of change was welcomed by many as a breath of fresh air. New hope was available that an Anglican church could be flexible without compromising essentials. For others, and not exclusively those of an older generation, the looseness of the group network, the experimenting with new modes of worship and the extent of the new inclusiveness[8] had already gone too far. Where was the orderly, predictable church they thought they once knew? Discontinuity, fragmentation and a fuzzy-edged faith was all they could see.

The legacy for the nineties, then, was this question: can the broad embrace of differing views that characterises Anglicanism as a *denomination* also be expressed in a *local congregation*?

PROFILE
BOB AND MOLLIE BROW
ROBERT BROW, RECTOR 1978-1989

Bob Brow was born in Karachi, Pakistan, in 1924, where his father was an engineer. He went to French school in Brussels and to schools in the South of England before entering officer training in South India. Commissioned with the Mahratta Light Infantry, he became adjutant of his battalion in Java before being demobilized in 1947.

While a student of economics and theology at Trinity College, Cambridge, Bob Brow forsook his former atheism to become a Christian, through the InterVarsity Group. He later returned to India to teach theology in Allahabad (for 11 years) and to be staff worker for the Union of Evangelical Students of India. He was ordained in Lucknow in 1953.

Mollie Tarrant had gone to India as a Baptist missionary nurse and midwife in 1952, and Bob and Mollie met in language school the next year. They were married in a tent within two hundred metres of the Nepal border, and all their four children were born in India.

The Brows came to Canada in 1964 when Bob began as North America Director of Interserve, a position he held for three years. Writing projects — in which Mollie shared — bore fruit during this period. The resulting books called for a new approach to missions, including the idea of "tentmaking," and to church life, and also discussed comparative religion.[9] Having studied earlier for his Th.M at Princeton Theological Seminary 1957-58, Bob was ready to undertake further study, this time in the linguistic philosophy of Wittgenstein, at the University of Toronto. He also taught in the Glendon College bilingual programme.

Parish service followed, first as rector of Cavan, 1971-75, then as assistant at Little Trinity, Toronto, 1975-78. The Brows arrived in Kingston in 1978, where, apart from some more recent short-term mission assignments, they have remained ever since. By the time they came, they were all set to try out some new ideas in their new charge, St James'. *Go Make Learners: A New Model for Discipleship in the Church* (Shaw, 1981) proposed that the church is at heart a school of the Holy Spirit, where people learn together what it means to live the Christian life. This book formed the manual that informed what Bob and Mollie attempted at St James'. They were also working towards what they now call "creative love theology," a fresh — and for some, a controversial — way of thinking about the "good news."[10]

Under their ministry the congregation of St James' grew and flourished, although they faced some difficult challenges. The Brows worked together, very much as a team, complementing each other with their different gifts. Both Bob and Mollie visited parishioners in their homes. The sense of a church not only as a school, but as a caring community was encouraged during their pastorate. Many groups mushroomed, the student cause was furthered and new forms of music and liturgy were introduced. The rectory door was open to all comers, providing a haven for some, a place of stimulus to service for others.

When they retired in 1989 the Brows went to live in the cottage Bob had built at Dog Lake, but they did not stop work! They have since been Interserve Associates in Paphos, Cyprus and Abu Dhabi in the United Arab Emirates and are currently leaders at Christchurch, Cataraqui back in Kingston. As well, they are now grandparents of nine children.

Bob Brow with seniors at the Christmas tea, 1988.

Bob Brow in a familiar role, 1987.

10

Facing The Future

"In a world of pain and fire and steel
Way out on the rim of a broken wheel."
— Bruce Cockburn[1]

The official story of the church dates from the erection of the building in 1845. If the fate of the church is bound up with its limestone structure, things may not look too bright. After many, many repairs to different parts of the building over the past fifteen decades, the weather-worn tower was finally declared unsafe in 1992. The top sections were pulled down and the amputated tower stump capped. The roof, suffering steadily since the addition of 1888, also required extensive repair. While the renovations have gone ahead, thanks largely to generous giving, the old stones are still vulnerable, and will cause trouble again.

The tower crisis of 1992 was seen by some, paradoxically, as a blessing in disguise. The building became a metaphor for thinking about where the church is going. As warden Jack Henderson put it, "God took us by the tower and shook." The crushing financial burden of repair, along with several practical questions about how people wanted the facility to look after renovation stimulated heart-searching, debate, and some discord. Why should one small group of people pay for a "heritage building" that has for a century-and-a-half enhanced the aesthetics of Kingston? Once the pews are out to allow floor repairs, should they be replaced with a flexible seating system more in tune with the times and with parish needs?

The symbolic "Ontario gothic" structure, standing on the Arch-Union corner for so long, is in jeopardy. The tower, that once set the architectural pace for development on Union Street,[2] can now be seen only in photos. Ironically, its latest grandchild, the Stauffer Library, was born in 1994, the year after its demise. A question mark hangs over whether or not the tower will rise again over Stuartville. But the bigger question concerns the structural condition of the church-as-people. Can the congregation withstand the weathering of cultural change, initiated in the 1960s, and still coming in unstable, unpredictable patterns, even as the turn of the century approaches?

Most of this book has looked at the past. We have surveyed the story of a church through the changing social and cultural landscapes of a hundred and fifty years. The closing chapter is far from a piece about endings, however! In what follows we turn from the past to the present and the future. Will the familiar building last? More importantly, what does a spiritual audit for the mid-1990s reveal? And what kind of prospects lie ahead; will St James' still be around in 2145?

ST JAMES' IN THE NINETIES

In the early nineties, the average congregation at 9:00 Sunday morning was about 40, and at 10.30, 160. Those households still on the church roll, and thus who still have some contact with St James', number 260 (see Appendix I). But numbers at meetings only tell part of the story. When Pat Patterson came as rector in 1990 he was warned that his first task would be

Just before the tower came down, 1991 (Janet Henderson).

Profile
PAT PATTERSON
RECTOR 1990-PRESENT

At New Year 1990 Pat Patterson became the ninth rector of St James' church. Born in Victoria, British Columbia in 1951, he first studied philosophy at the University of Victoria before enrolling at Wycliffe Hall Theological College in Oxford, England. There he was joined by his wife, Rose, also a "UVic" graduate. His first curacy was at St Andrew's, Bebington, Merseyside, following his ordination as deacon at Chester Cathedral in 1976.

Patterson's first contact with the Irish connection was not at St James' but at St John's, Shaughnessy, Vancouver, where he served as associate rector to Harry Robinson, a prominent bearer of that tradition.[3] While Patterson shares a firm commitment to biblical preaching, he describes himself as a "Catholic evangelical," a term that would have mystified if not raised the neck-hairs of St James' founders! Times have changed!

He was rector of St John's, Duncan, B.C. from 1983 to 1989. He came to St James' with his family, which by now included three daughters, Gina, Lara and Nicola. The challenge of a church on Queen's campus was, for him, the primary attraction to St James'. Little did he know that within a short period of time other major challenges would confront him and the church, both personal ones and the tower crisis of 1992, and its aftermath.

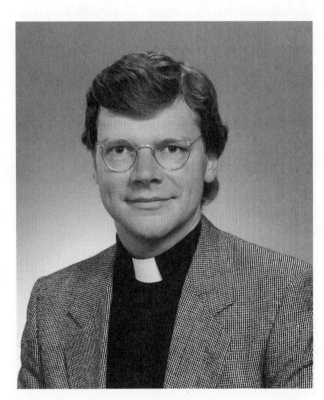

Pat Patterson,
St James' rector
since 1990.

to try to coordinate various splinters that were in danger of breaking off into their own orbit. Because this mandate was read by some as a desire to control, Patterson's early period at St James' was not without tension.

More than one compromise solution currently holds things together. Both the Book of Common Prayer and Book of Alternative Services are used, at different services. Music at 10:30 is led by both organ-and-choir plus the music group, using guitar, violin, flute and piano. Evening Prayer on Sunday (now discontinued) and Morning Prayer each day attract a handful only. By contrast, a monthly Sunday evening "Gathering" for experimental and contemporary worship has drawn up to 150, many from other churches.

During the 1990s, long-term features such as the Wednesday communion and breakfast or the Seder Supper on Good Friday have continued. Alongside them, new initiatives, especially involving younger people, have begun to flourish. The vision and energy of Paul Walker has much to do with their success.[4] He is the supposedly "part-time" rector's assistant, and is a layperson. The "7:11" group of teens meets weekly and also takes canoe, bike and hiking trips from time-to-time. The Sunday School has also been split into age-groups clubs, NUTTs, STEPs and TUFs.

Again, support for missionary work has continued, particularly in respect of Pam Hunt, working in Manila, Philippines. But the realities of overseas mission were brought home even

Pam Hunt, missionary teacher in the Philippines, 1990.

A dramatic scene as the St James' tower is dismantled in 1992. Queen's, KGH buildings and the lake are visible behind (*Whig-Standard*).

Replacing the roof of St James', 1993
(*Whig-Standard*).

Honduras
Project '93
team members,
Tegucigalpa.

more vividly when a St James' team of thirteen went to Honduras for the summer of 1993. They joined Roger Hurtubise, a South American Missionary Society worker, in the village of Coral Quemado, near Tegucigalpa.

Helping in practical building projects and learning to sing worship songs in Spanish meant that many stories were brought back to give the church a sense of being part of a much bigger world. As one team-member said, "It was a real privilege to be present with the church in Honduras; [a situation] so different from what I am used to, *and* to feel we were doing something useful . . . ."[5]

Groups such as the Sanctuary Guild and the Craft Group go on with their tasks, and two home groups, meeting for Bible study and prayer also still thrive. The group of parents — mainly mothers — who meet weekly to discuss and pray together, serves a useful function in drawing people into the church and of support or reassurance for those on the margins.[6] Adult education classes have also begun, to encourage more in-depth understanding of Christian roots and of the demands of discipleship.

At the same time, other issues, other groups, other areas receive less attention. One unresolved matter concerns women-and-men. The growing openness of the eighties towards the concerns of women and their involvement in leadership was replaced in the nineties with uncertainty at best, and felt rejection, at worst. One of the happiest periods in this regard was when Devona Wiederick shared ministerial tasks with Pat Patterson in 1992 and 1993. How the church will find a way fully to include women in every aspect of congregational life remains to be seen.

Not all that the 1979 mission statement aspired to has been achieved. Who knows how long the 1993 version will command support? Some faithful members have left the church, even as newcomers have joined in. Yet others hover on the fringes, or think of themselves as St James' people without actually attending events. Many regulars are very content, others would like to see things done differently. Is this inevitable, or does it reflect some larger trends in church and society?

TAKING STOCK

During 1993 and 1994 much thought was given to a "strategic plan" and a "mission statement" for the parish.[7] Questions asked of parishioners, and ensuing discussions, produced a number of revealing reflections of where the church is now and where it is going. Although the survey was very open, and the sample of those responding fairly random, some strong impressions may be gleaned from it. At certain crucial points it is fair to claim that widespread agreement exists.

People enjoy being at St James', apparently, because of the sense of community experienced there. Many words are used to describe it: family, belonging, fellowship being the three

Frontenac Park canoe trip, April 1994.

Members of the St James' congregation,
January 1995 (Janet Henderson).

most frequently used. They cite the welcome they received or the sense of being accepted for who they are. They mention the home group, the Camp Iawah retreats or the Wednesday communion and breakfast as examples of where this can be felt. They value the quality and commitment of "lay" leadership. Or they say how someone invited them back to their home; hospitality is seen as a big plus.

For many who warmly recall the eighties, there is also a sense of accepting others; street people, women-in-ministry, students. Tolerance for all within a diverse community is felt to be very important. The very fact that at St James' all the different age groups are represented is an attraction. Others are pleased that St James' accommodates a large proportion of people from non-Anglican backgrounds; Christian Reformed, Alliance, Brethren, Mennonite, Baptist, Catholic, Pentecostal and so on. Yet others note that St James' is not solidly WASP (White Anglo-Saxon Protestant) either!

While the sense of community is strong, it also has some specific reference points. Evangelical, biblical, concern about the meaningfulness of worship, these are sentiments that crop up constantly. The serious way in which "scriptures are opened up" is how someone expressed their approval. Repeatedly, thoughtful preaching and teaching is cited as a St James' distinctive. It seems that people who come to St James' want a demanding, challenging, relevant stimulus that affects their daily lives.

While a minority may be impatient with *certain* hymns or songs, most people say they like the balance between the traditional and the contemporary in worship. This also includes the sense of continuity with the past that comes from using liturgical forms from the prayer books. Many point to practices such as kneeling for prayer or frequent communion as means of demonstrating seriousness of intent and a desire to see worship as distinct from the lightness and triviality of contemporary TV and consumerism.

But even these reference points are not enough. As a means of stating what *kind* of community exists and is cherished at St James' they fill out the picture. But those who completed the forms consistently pointed to the "vertical" dimension — Godward — not just the "horizontal" — person-to-person — as being crucial.[8] Words like "Christ-centred" appeared repeatedly, as did a stress on the gospel of the cross, emphasized again in appreciation of the Lord's Supper.

Interestingly enough, this connects right back to the roots of St James', albeit now modified by time. Despite its bad name in some quarters, evangelicalism has persisted as an emphasis on the Bible, the cross, conversion and activism in outreach.[9] More recently, stress has also been placed on fellowship and the ministry of all members, which again links back to nineteenth century lay-leadership. Though they may reject the evangelical label, these concerns are also more prominent within broader Anglican — and other denominational — circles today.

St James' Mission Statement: We, the community of St James' Anglican Church, seek to glorify God through our worship and ministry. Rooted in the Word of God, nurtured by prayer and sacrament, and guided by the Holy Spirit, we desire to learn and apply all that Jesus would teach us. We are challenged to accept and value each person; to love, encourage and affirm one another as members of a caring family; to discover, develop and share our gifts and ministries; to grow in faith; and to live and spread the Gospel. United in the Body of Christ, we celebrate our diversity and strive to response to the special needs within our congregation, the Queen's community, and our neighbours beyond.

Needless to say, however, the findings of the survey were not uniformly positive! Some feel that the different age-and-interest cohorts are competing rather than cooperating. Some feel a sense of failure because a number of people left in the early nineties and they have not been persuaded to return. The issue over which they left was a sense that the church had shifted abruptly away from participation and back to hierarchy. Women especially had experienced this very negatively.

Others would like to see more prayer, more outreach, more concern for seniors, more responsibility taken by a bigger proportion of the congregation. Still others would like to see the tower firmly back in place! What happens in each of these areas remains to be seen. Nonetheless, St James' *did* commit itself to a Mission Statement in 1994.

ANGLICANISM TODAY

Once, the Anglican centre of gravity was in England, and the Canadas were peripheral cousins. Eventually, the Anglican Church of Canada took responsibility for its own future. This independence meant that it tended in a more Protestant direction of a national church rather than seeking the Roman Catholic supranational ideal. Lay involvement in leadership strengthened this tendency. The centre of Canadian Anglicanism moved away from Kingston a long time ago. But St James' was involved in both shifts and remains part of the Anglican communion today, locally, nationally, and globally. This has several implications.

Globally, while Anglicanism is declining in the UK, USA, Canada, Australia and New Zealand, it is still growing in African countries and in Papua New Guinea. This is a healthy sign for Anglicanism in general, but could obscure the extent of loss in countries where traditionally it was strong. Its failing strength is in some ways analogous to that of the Commonwealth.

Despite the relative independence of the Anglican Church in Canada, it is still connected in many minds with Britain. The loyalism of a Dr Naughton exemplifies this older but partly persisting attitude. So some Canadians who might identify themselves as Anglicans do so because of their attachment to British roots rather than their commitment to a congregation or to Christ.[10] But this is hardly true of St James' in the nineties.

In Canada, church leaders are confronted with rapidly declining numbers. After 70 years of steady growth, Anglican membership nose-dived from 1,300,000 in 1960 to 800,000 in 1990.[11] Against this backdrop, St James' ailments appear benign. Other mainline denominations face the same gloomy statistics. In 1993 36% of the Canadian population claimed allegiance to a Protestant church compared with 56% in 1921.[12] Only newcomers such as Pentecostalism are growing.

Globally, Anglicanism is also in trouble because its membership is topheavy in terms of age. Difficulties with keeping young people are endemic. Likewise, it tends to be badly gender unbalanced, with a preponderance of women sometimes around 2:1. The exceptions lie in evangelical congregations, and St James' provides a good example of this. Other Anglicans in the diocese often express surprise both at the male-female balance and at the apparent capacity of St James' to offer something to young people. The presence of students may distort this data somewhat, but it is true that the young people's work at St James' is in relatively good shape.

St James' was crucially involved in the growth of Canadian evangelical Anglicanism in the nineteenth century. It should be no surprise,

then, that St James' sent the biggest group of members in the diocese to the major "Anglican Essentials" conference in Montreal in June 1994. The meeting drew over 700 to a five-day meeting to thrash out in small groups and huge plenaries what is vital to Anglican belief and practice in the 1990s. It also drew together people concerned about the prayer book, with renewal, and with active parish life.[13] Again, all three emphases may be discerned at St James' today.

ISSUES CONFRONTING THE CHURCH

To date, St James' has been spared the fate of many churches. While members — rightly — may be grateful, it is no cause for complacency. The special circumstances of a church on the campus, with strongly committed lay leaders and a robust biblical tradition have done much to help. But we should note that the dismal decline in churchgoing that characterises all mainline denominations is part of a significant paradox. The emptying pews do not signal a rejection of religion. Rather, it seems that Canadians are seeking the sacred elsewhere. And while a minority plumps for New Age, native spirituality, or another conventional religion, most claim commitment to Christian belief of a strikingly orthodox kind.[14]

One crucial issue confronting the church, then, is the phenomenon of "believing without belonging."[15] The problem here is not so much non-belief as non-membership. Having said that, of course, it must be only a matter of time before

Parading to a service in City Park, June 1991 (Janet Henderson).

belief also becomes diffused and diluted to the point that its resemblance to Christian faith is only faint. Moreover, to claim to believe certain ideas about God or Jesus does not constitute "discipleship" in the strong sense used, for example, by Bob Brow. Nonetheless, however "secular" the current context may appear, it is far from fully "post-Christian," still less "non-religious."

So what can St James' — and by the same token any church — do to reclaim what seems to be lost ground? The story of a church is hardly the place to go into questions of future strategy in detail. But on the other hand, the peculiar trajectory of this particular church seems to demand that attention be paid to the question. The best way is to revisit the internal attempts to seek direction for the church. As we saw, these were sparked by the tower crisis, and have led to a fresh focus on three areas; outreach, community and ministries.[16]

Churches that grow, it seems, believe in growing. They are unsatisfied with only holding operations or maintenance as strategies. A significant St James' group has been working with Wycliffe's Harold Percy to consider how the church can be more user-friendly and outreach-oriented. This is directly in line with the leading tradition at St James', expressed variously in Robert Rogers' or Desmond Hunt's calls for conversion or the parish plan of 1979. The tension here will be between loyalty to the Anglican denomination and the offer of a Christian spirituality expressed in Anglican ways.

Small groups, and indeed anything that fosters that elusive "sense of community," are a second

St James' dwarfed by campus buildings, winter 1995 (Abi Lyon).

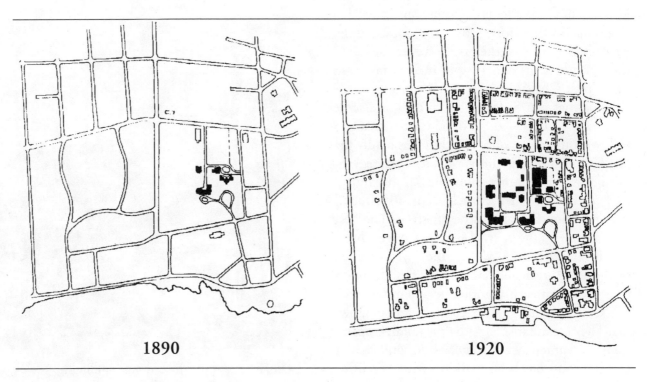

1890   **1920**

Queen's campus plan maps show clearly
the growing predominance of university
buildings in St James' parish. The map
on page 24 shows residential housing
that existed well before 1890.

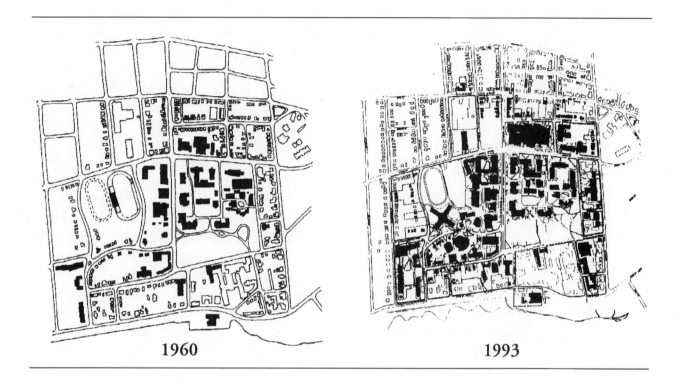

1960   **1993**

crucial component of churches that are doing well in the 1990s. This has been a vital aspect of life at St James' since the 1960s and echoes the extensive lay-involvement that was woven into the fabric of St James' since the start. It is a healthy sign that community building is seen as a high priority in the survey of church opinion. The danger here is the converse of the one mentioned before; "belonging without believing." Various studies have shown that classic Christian commitments are easily reduced to a cosy quest for togetherness when members lose sight of the bigger — biblical — picture of "fellowship."[17]

Thirdly, St James' has tried to work out what are the special ministries offered by the church. From 1993, the annual budget began to be "ministry-based."[18] This could also be thought of in terms of the particular needs that St James' can attempt to address. Student work at Queen's is perhaps the most obvious, but others, to seniors, to parents-and-families, and to people struggling with the demands of daily involvement in business, academic life and management, call for attention. The task here entails distinguishing between a mere consumer approach, in which the church markets an array of services, on the one hand, and a matching of congregational gifts with strategic learning and action appropriate to the contemporary world, on the other.

Cutting across all three areas will be the ongoing issue of gender. Questions about the theology of God or the ordination of women are just symptoms of the larger shifts taking place today. Gender and sexuality are increasingly becoming the litmus test for biblical faithfulness and for adequate encounter with today's world. These issues will not go away, and the quality of Christian life at St James', as elsewhere, will be judged on how they are handled.

The current domestic reassessment of roles must also occur in the church, in the light of the imperative that women share in leadership and of the movement of more women into paid work. Until the 1960s, as we have seen, such women were leaders in two critical areas, missions and fundraising. Similarly, St James' can no longer assume that clergy wives — like the well-loved Naomi Hunt or Mollie Brow — will automatically take a full, unpaid share in their husbands' work.[19] Or, for that matter, that clergy husbands will do so. The health of the church may be more dependent than we know on the quality of partnership in ministry.[20]

In terms of her heritage, St James' may well be obliged to ask how well she continues three traditions. One is the desire to be biblical people. Early "laypeople" knew clearly what they believed and why. They could connect their faith with scripture. But far fewer people are now exposed to systematic, long-term ways of learning what is Christian faith. And too often the churches seek "expertise" from whatever source, rather than doing the biblical homework of our forebears in order authentically to confront the contemporary world.

The second tradition is concern for the marginalised. The story of the church could be read as "from poverty to privilege." It would be a betrayal of St James' heritage if today's church failed to follow the lead of Rogers, Kirkpatrick and many others. They saw active and practical neighbour-love as a vital sign of true Christian commitment. Their biblical stress could be called holistic spirituality. Social concern and commitment to the cross of Christ were seen as close partners.

The third tradition is a strong sense of identity. Lacking the old taken-for-granted evangelical culture, what is the task of the church today? Without a doubt, churches that survive will be outward-looking. The story of St James' shows that vision — such as for Canada as God's dominion — and mission — often done with others — has given the sense of unity and identity to the church. Conversely, when vision has been dimmed, or when (comm)unity has been sought for its own sake, a sense of identity and purpose has been obscured.

THE CHURCH ON THE CAMPUS

One aspect of St James' identity will continue to be her relation to Queen's. Gone are the days when the connections were obvious, when church and university were just different manifestations of a culture deeply influenced by Christianity. St James' no longer invites the principal to speak at the church, Queen's no longer thinks of including the St James' rector among the candidates for honorary doctorates.

This is not just an institutional but a cultural matter. By mid-century, the old liaison was breaking down between faith and reason, once a shared commitment on campus and at church. More and more, modern science left little place for faith. Believing professors kept their religion in a private compartment while practising "neutral" disciplines. This even applied in theology. Meanwhile, after the sixties and seventies, open hostility against the churches was sometimes expressed, often fuelled by anger against sexism, abuse or cultural imperialism.

Another major shift is taking place in the 1990s, however, which alters the field beyond recognition. Alongside a pluralism that rightly insists that no special privileges should be given to any one religious group is a radical questioning of the assumptions of "modern reason." "Hard science" turns out to have a soft core; modernity itself comes to be seen as provisional. While the postmodern turn[21] may come slowly at Queen's, its effects will be no less profound. If this story tried to trace the intertwined trails of religion and modernity, the emerging mood reappraises both.

The challenge to a church on the campus is to reconsider the role of religious commitments. How far have they been allowed to rest on a false philosophical foundation?[22] How far does the stained record of the churches disable future efforts aimed at social welfare or education? The opportunities opening before the church are equally tremendous: to take advantage of the new mood to indicate the ways that commitments affect intellectual activity and to speak of faith in a new climate that values symbolism and spirituality.

Such challenges and opportunities are not limited to St James' and Queen's campus, of course. Canadian and indeed global cultures are affected in various ways by the same trends. I mention them here only because a church like St James' is particularly well-placed to interact with them. St James' has thus far managed to avoid both extremes of fundamentalism (anti-modern reaction) and liberalism (the embrace of modernism). Pursuing a middle way is not just an Anglican quirk. It may provide a model for engaging with the postmodern world.

STUARTVILLE: PAST MEMORY;
QUEEN'S CAMPUS: PRESENT REALITY

In 1845, all the lay leaders were local artisans and small business owners. They chiselled building stones, made furniture, brewed beer, supplied or sailed ships and dug gardens. They were mainly Irish settlers and none was well off. In 1995, the contrast could not be more complete. Recent wardens have been mainly employed by or directly connected with Queen's; a communications manager, professors of computing, chemistry, medicine. None was born in Kingston (or Ireland!) and none is poor.

Contrasts there may be, but also continuities. Is it an accident that Robert Rogers, rector in 1845, may have come from the Cambridge of Charles Simeon, who dreamed of declaring the Good News within the heart of the university? Was it coincidence that the rector who oversaw the post-war golden years at St James' wore the mantle of Irish evangelical Anglicanism, a century after it took root in Kingston? Is it not symbolic that IVCF was founded within a campus church like St James'?

What do such continuities within contrasts tell us? That the building is not a mere museum for a bygone culture. And that the church that meets in the building is more than an abiding social institution or a voluntary organization. Because it is at least these things, tomorrow's congregation still must respect the traditions of the past *and* be actively involved in working out fresh ways forward for the future. But because it is more, churchpeople can live confidently today, in hope that is reinforced by revived memory.[23]

Naturally we are grateful for the people who we discover as our forebears in the faith. We can delight in their dedication, weep with their struggles, laugh at their incongruities, admire their courage, cringe at their mistakes, distance ourselves from their disputes. But the story of St James' Church does not allow us to stop there.

The "living stones" of this story, knowing that their roles are specific, limited, and flawed, point beyond themselves to the architect and builder in whom alone the story makes sense, and for whom the story becomes a joyful song.

The following graphs indicate some of the main changes at St James' over the past 150 years. While not all the figures are readily available, we have enough to get a general overview. It must be stressed, therefore, that while consistency has been sought, the uneven quality of the original data limits the accuracy of the graphs.

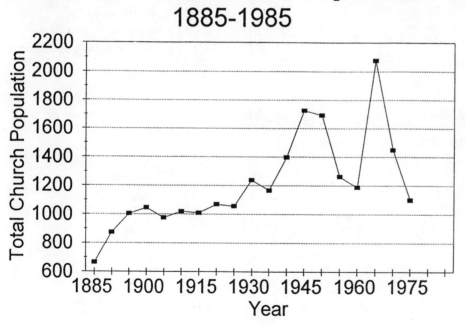

Total St. James' Population
1885-1985

Figure 1 indicates the number of people attached to the parish between 1885 and 1975, according to the register of households recorded by the diocese. From this perspective the so-called golden years of the late fifties and early sixties stand out. Actual church attendance figures, though available, are counted differently in different decades (one service or two, etc.) so that we just have no way of knowing exactly how many people were in church over a period of time.

Canadian Anglican Membership
1926-85

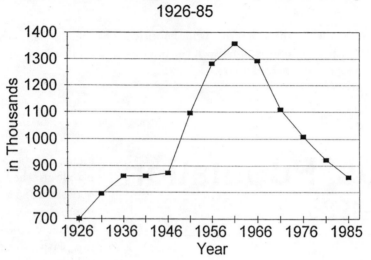

Figure 2 shows Canadian Anglican membership, as calculated by Reginald Bibby (*Unknown Gods: The Ongoing Story of Religion in Canada*, Don Mills, Stoddart, 1993), for the years 1926–1985, while Figure 3 puts this in the context of the Canadian population as a whole.

Anglican Membership 1926-85
as % total Canadian population

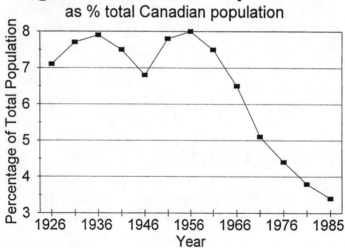

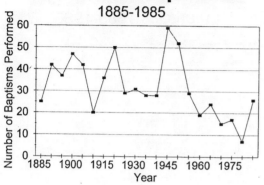

St. James' Baptisms
1885-1985

Figures 4, 5, and 6 show population shifts in terms of rites of passage. Most remarkable here is evidence of the wartime baby booms. It is interesting that marriage does not seem to have been popular at St James' during the Depression.

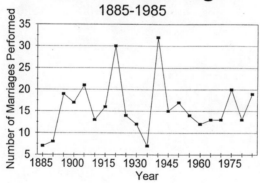

St. James' Marriages
1885-1985

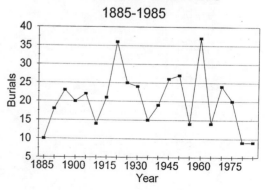

St. James' Burials
1885-1985

St. James' Vital Statistics
Sunday School Statistics 1885-1980

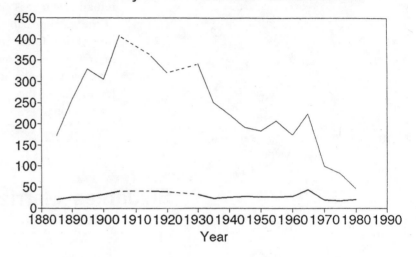

Figure 7 shows just how significant
an institution the Sunday School
was from the turn-of-the-century
until World War II. The temporary
upturn in the sixties and seventies
relates directly to the baby boom
shown in Figure 4. The broken
lines indicate a lack of data.

Average Giving
Per Communicant

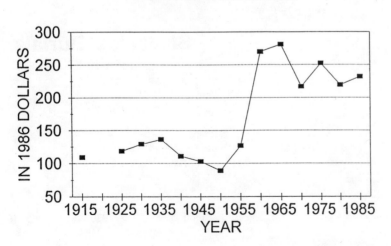

Figure 8 is the average giving per communicant
from 1915–1985. It is interesting to note that
among the confirmed membership of St James'
average giving in 1988 was $633.38 per capita
(= $139,979 divided by total communicants, 221),
compared with the national Anglican figure of
$342.48 per capita. (If this method of computing
is thought artificially to inflate the figure, even
substituting total population still produces
$437.44.) Among Baptist Convention churches
the equivalent figure is $1,016.74 but for the
United Church of Canada $308.97. (*The Yearbook
of American and Canadian Churches*, Nashville TN:
Abingdon Press, 1990, p. 268.)

Total Expenditures

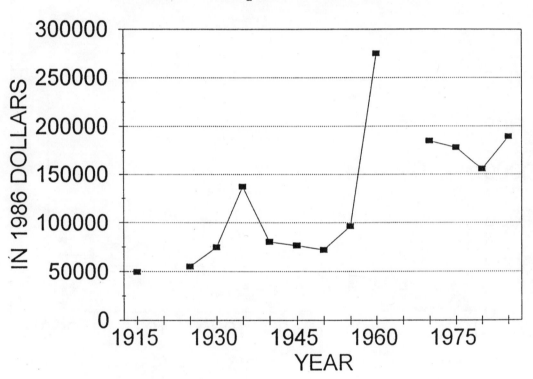

Figure 9 shows the total expenditures for St James', 1915–1985. From 1911 it was possible to adjust for inflation (see note below), which is why these dates apply. They can be expressed in 1986 Canadian dollars. By comparing this with Figure 10 (expenditure breakdown by category) some of the movement in the graph can be explained. The sharp rise in expenditures in the 1930s and 1960s, for example, reflects building renovations (and shows what a mixed blessing is "heritage building ownership?) It should be noted that from the late 1950s to the early 1970s spending was greater on mission and salaries as well as maintenance. As with all these statistics, warnings must be heeded about the inadequacy and inconsistency of the original data.

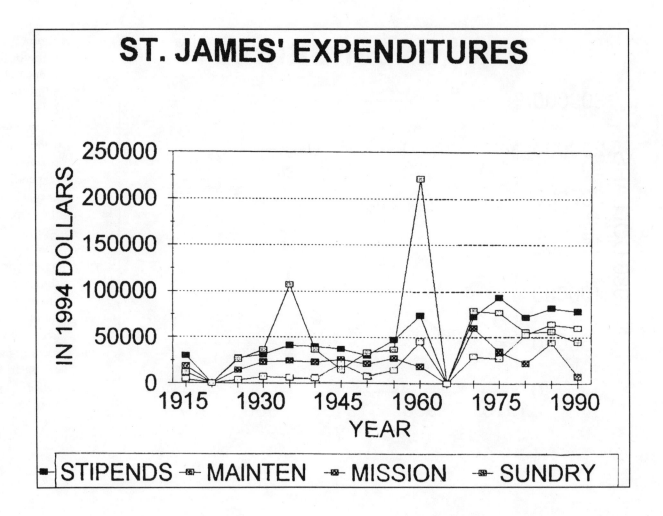

*The Consumer Price Index (CPI) began in 1911, which is why these tables start in 1915. In 1986 the CPI+100; thus the formula was 100 x (CPI, year X)/($given).

The four categories used for the expenditure breakdown sometimes required judgement such as when accounts were conflated. Other accounts, such as WA and Sunday School, are omitted because they were separate. *Stipends* include salaries for the rector, rector's assistant, organist, sexton and pulpit supply. *Maintenance* includes building costs, utilities, fuel, interest, debt, insurance, taxes. *Missions* includes outreach events, donations and costs incurred by the Sunday School. *Sundries* includes printing, choir books, communion wine, radio broadcasts, advertising, Synod apportionment (after 1980 this became a major expenditure).

Data is taken primarily from St James' financial statements, though some missing figures had to be gleaned from *Synod Journal* reports. Rental of church property is not included in giving, which refers to freewill offerings.

"Communicants" is the nearest thing to "membership" in the Anglican fold, but even this is inexact. It is assumed that this represents confirmed or self-designated adherents. Data is obtained from the *Synod Journal* reports, although because figures were missing for 1880 and 1925, those of 1883 and 1926 are used instead.

Appendix Two

These are the rectors, vicars, curates, assistants and wardens who have served St James' Church since 1845.

RECTORS OF ST JAMES' CHURCH

Robert Vashon Rogers	(1843) 1845–1869
Francis Kirkpatrick	1869–1885
John Kerr McMorine	1885–1909
Thomas W. Savery	1912–1930
John MacKenzie-Naughton	1931–1953
Desmond Hunt	1953–1969
Gordon Hendra	1969–1978
Robert Brow	1978–1989
Patrick D.M. Patterson	1990–

ASSISTANT MINISTERS OF ST. JAMES' CHURCH

W.B. Moffatt	1868
John H.H. Coleman	1893–1895; 1898–1900
Richard Coleman	1895–1896
Thomas W. Savary	1901–1903
C.K. Masters	1903–1905
C.L. Bilkey	1906–1909
Thomas W. Savary (Vicar)	1909–1912
A.C. McCullum (Assistant)	1960?
Raymond Carder	1960–1962
James Slater (Curate)	1964–1967
Charles Montizambert (Curate)	1968
Jean Boyd (Parish Worker)	1968–1969
Eric Howes (Curate)	1974–1976
Douglass Ray (Assistant)	1976–1978
Keith Jones(Assistant)	
Marie Warner	1976–1979
Lee Huddleston	1980
David Ward (Curate)	1984–1986
Paul Walker (Rector's Assistant)	1991–1995
Devona Wiederick	1993–1994

CHURCH WARDENS OF ST. JAMES' CHURCH

Hon. P.B. deBlaquiere	1845
Micah Mason	1845–1846
G. Gilmore	1846
Dr. A.C. Robertson	1847
Fred Kaylor	1847
H. Dupuy	1848–1850
Thomas Mostyn	1848
Neil McLeod	1849–1853
William Rudston	1851–1856
Dr. Hayward	1854
Abraham Foster	1856–1858
Anthony J. O'Loughlin	1857–1858
T. Coxworthy	1859
J. Rowlands	1859
W.P. Street	1860–1863
William Shannon	1860–1866; 1869; 1870
Edward Horsey	1864
Ray S. Vaughan	1865–1868
E.R. Welch	1867–1868
R. Kent	1869–1870
Robert V. Rogers	1871–1875; 1881; 1886–1895
Peter Bates	1871–1876; 1883–1885
G. Durnford	1876–1880
Edward J.B. Pense	1877–1882; 1886–1895
Shore Loynes	1882–1885
H. Dupuy	1896
J.S.R. McCann	1896–1897; 1906
R.J. Hooper	1897–1900
J.A. Drummond	1898–1900
George E. Hague	1901–1905; 1920–1927
Francis King	1901–1911

W.J.C. Allen	1907–1910	Dr. R.N. Green	1972–1973
J.R. Forster	1911–1912	William Wright	1974–1977
H.H. Taylor	1912–1913	Dr. Ross Beardall	1974–1975
William H. Dalby	1913–1915	Jack Grenville	1976–1977
H. Sharpe	1914–1915; 1928–1931	Dr. Stanley Jarzylo	1978–1979
W.N. Linton	1916–1917	Paul Speight	1978–1979
J. Farrar	1916–1918	John (Jack) Pike	1980–1981
S.C. Smith	1918–1920	Irene Cleland	1980–1983
J.K. Carroll	1919	David Manning	1982–1983
W.J. Saunders	1921–1923	Evans Davis	1983–1984
Prof. L.T. Rutledge	1924–1925	Bruce Pond	1984–1985
Dr. P.H. Huyck	1926–1927; 1942–	William Blenkinsop	1985–1986
Fred C. Reid	1928–1934	Lois Armstrong	1986–1987
H.B. Sandwith	1932–1936; 1946–1949	David Rhind	1987–1988
A. Drew	1935–1938	Ross Wilkins	1989–1990
J.S.M. Sharpe	1937–1940	Irene Cleland	1990
A.C. Baldwin	1939–1941	James Peters	1989–1991
E.L. Earl	1941–1943	Jack Watson	1989–1992
James Breen	1946–1953	George Hay	1991–1993
J.E. Whiting	1950–1957	Susan Abell	1992–1993
Prof. R.G. Smails	1954–1957	John (Jack) Hendersen	1992–1995
Harold Ripley	1958–1969	Dr. Pam Frid	1994
Dr. Kenneth Fryer	1958–1959	David Lamb	1994–
Harry Juby	1960–1971	Dr. Irene Swift	1995–
George Clarke	1970–1973		

Notes

The following references are full as possible. However, as some of the St James' archival material has yet to be processed at the Diocesan Archives I have listed no specific box number.

Chapter One

1. Bill Barnes, "Formal Prose" from *Complex Variables: Poems and Music by William John Barnes*, ed. David Helwig and Peter Taylor, Kingston: Quarry Press, 1994, p. 15.

2. No doubt this was soon after Rogers' return to Kingston. The waterways would have had to be open for him to arrive, and presumably some time was spent organizing the meeting place and gathering the group together.

3. Sermon by Rogers preached at Mason's funeral and reported in *The Berean*, December 16, 1847.

4. The announcement that a "free church" would start on Sunday, June 25, 1843 was made by George Okill Stuart, and the "Line Barracks School" was the meeting place (DOA 4KM2). The 1945 anniversary booklet suggests only that the church met in the Midland District School before moving to other temporary premises.

5. I shall use "Anglican" as a shorthand for the United Church of England and Ireland even though the term would not come into use until later.

6. See George Rawlyk, *The Canada Fire: Radical Evangelicalism in British North America 1775–1812*, Kingston and Montreal: McGill-Queen's University Press, 1994, pp. 103-105.

7. For background see David Hempton and Myrtle Hill, *Evangelical Protestantism in Ulster Society 1740-1890*, London and New York: Routledge, 1992.

8. Donald Akenson, *The Irish in Ontario*, Kingston and Montreal: McGill-Queen's, 1991, chapter 1.

9. Alternatively, the O'Loughlin family history may have got Anthony's arrival date wrong.

10. Other members of the building committee were Charles Willard, Micah Mason (who, along with the Hon. P.B. de Blaquiere became the first warden), Samuel Mucklestone, and John Macaulay. At the first vestry meeting in 1845 Stafford Lightbourne, succeeding head of the Midland District School, was appointed vestry clerk.

11. See William Westfall, *Two Worlds: The Protestant Culture of Nineteenth Century Ontario*, Kingston and Montreal: McGill-Queen's University Press, 1989, chapter 5, "Epics in Stone."

12. See Jennifer McKendry, *William Coverdale and the architecture of Kingston from 1835-1865*, PhD Thesis, University of Toronto, 1991. It is noteworthy that Little Trinity Church in Toronto, with its very similar English and Irish Protestant founders, never did construct a chancel.

13. *The Berean*, December 16 1847.

14. 1945 booklet, Kirkpatrick reminiscence (DOA).

15. Allan Anderson, *The Anglican Churches of Kingston*, 1963, p. 47.

16. Donald Schurman, *A Bishop and his People: John Travers Lewis and the Anglican Diocese of Ontario 1862-1902*, Kingston: Ontario Diocesan Synod, 1991, pp. 11–18 and Curtis Fahey, *In His Name: The Anglican Experience in Upper Canada 1791– 1854*, Ottawa: Carleton University Press, 1991, pp. 64-68.

17. See Fahey, chapter 7.

18. Tulchinsky in Brian Osborne and Donald Swainson *Kingston: Building on the Past*, Westport: Butternut Press, 1988, p. 118.

19. See, e.g., William J. Patterson, *Courage, Faith and Love: The History of St Mark's Church, Barriefield, Ontario*, Barriefield: St Mark's, 1993.

20. Rogers was a leading figure in the attempted local Anglican autonomy of Kingston in the 1850s, and this sometimes involved trying to maintain links with England. (See Donald Schurman, chapter four.) Rogers' reasons for this, one suspects, were not so much respect for colonial power as a desire for doctrinal purity in the new church.

21. James Roy's history of Kingston gave George Okill Stuart some bad press, and this is not downplayed, e.g., Osborne and Swainson, p.118– 119. He did participate in worthy causes, from the Bible Society to the General Hospital. But if he had not opposed the incorporation of Stuartville, arguably the area would have been cleaned up sooner than it was, though no doubt with some loss of rental income to him.

22. Quoted Osborne and Swainson p. 119.

23. Register of baptisms 1845, Box 4-K-1.

24. At an 1839 meeting in Bytown, for instance, he had been among those opposing the "persecution" of the church by the governing authorities. See Fahey, p. 83.

25. From the original announcement of meetings in the new building, 1845.

26. Reported in *The Berean*, February 8, 1849.

27. *Building Blocks of Kingston*, p. 12.

28. See, e.g., Douglas Johnson, *Contending for the Faith*, Leicester: IVP, 1979 p. 32ff.

29. In the 1830s, Simeon routinely sent promising young men to his friend Bishop McIlvaine in Ohio, whom he had met in 1830. Whether he already did this before then I do not know.

30. What the potential conflicts at Kenyon College would have been is unclear. The matter is mentioned in *Home Words*, September 1886.

31. Quoted in *Home Words*, September 1886.

32. *Journals of the Legislative Assembly*, Toronto, 1841, appendix M, quoted in McKendry, *op. cit.*, p. 40.

33. *The Berean*, IV, 38, Dec 16 1847.

34. Announcement, *op. cit.*

35. Letter of reply to the gift and memorial of 1863.

36. Allen P. Stouffer, *The Light of Nature and the Law of God*, Montreal and Kingston: McGill-Queen's University Press, 1992, p. 149

37. Quoted in Fred Laudon, "The Anti-Slavery Society of Canada" *Ontario History*, 48, 1956, pp. 125–132.

38. See Fahey, p. 259–265.

39. From a letter written by Robert O'Loughlin of Bronxville, NY in 1963.

Chapter Two

1. Jane Urquhart, *Away*, Toronto: McClelland and Stewart, 1993, p. 211.

2. One wonders whether or not Givins (sometimes spelled Givens) intended to give offence. Curtis Fahey claims he was an evangelical. He had been a missionary to the Mohawk village in the Bay of Quinte from 1833–1850 (see Curtis Fahey, *In His Name*, Ottawa: Carleton University Press, 1991, p. 44). In 1849 he had moved a resolution at the Church Society that the organization agree that "the evident duty of every member of the Church of England is to study the Word of God, in order to discover what the precise will of God at this time is . . ." *The Berean*, March 1 1849, p. 194. On the other hand, as Shirley Spragge observed to me, Givins was taught by John Strachan, studied at Trinity College, and preached at Bishop Bethune's funeral, none of which tallies with an evangelical outlook!

3. Centenary Booklet p. 10.

4. Anderson, *The Anglican Churches of Kingston*, p. 51. Comer, whose resolution it was, moved to Kingston from Niagara region in 1849. Details from his son, George's diary, now held by Mrs Betty White.

5. See Donald Schurman, "Scandal at St George's" in Donald Swainson (ed.) *St George's Cathedral: Two Hundred Years of Community*, Kingston: Quarry Press, 1991.

6. St James' Vestry Minutes, April 6, 1863. There may be something in the charge made by Donald Schurman that Rogers "was a fractious man who had once written rudely to the bishop and incurred his wrath." See "Bishop Strachan and the archdeaconry of Kingston, 1840–1846", *Historic Kingston*, 8, November 1959, p. 29. But my sense is that while Rogers was outspoken about his convictions, he was self-controlled.

7. Letter acknowledging anniversary gift, 1863.

8. Printed in *The Berean*, April 16 1846.

9. Compare the account of D.C. Masters, "Anglican Evangelicals in Toronto," *Journal of the Canadian Church Historical Society*, 20:3-4, 1978.

10. Sermon at St James' July 12 1846, printed in *The Berean*, August 27 1846.

11. Osborne and Swainson p. 246.

12. Osborne and Swainson p. 109.

13. Osborne and Swainson p. 268.

14. Margaret Cohoe, "Shannon's Cannon," *Historic Kingston*, 22, March 1974, p. 60.

15. *A Chronological Outline of the Life of Anthony J. O'Loughlin*, unpublished document, owned by his descendants.

16. Anne McDiarmid, "The visit of the Prince of Wales to Kingston," *Historic Kingston*, 21, 19 , pp. 50-61.

17. The chair eventually found a home in St Anthony's Chapel, Yarker, Ontario, which was erected in 1895 in memory of Anthony O'Loughlin, where it was referred to as the "bishop's chair." It is now at St Peter's, Harrowsmith.

18. See Margaret Cohoe, pp. 60-63.

19. This is the conclusion of the July 12 1846 sermon, *The Berean*.

20. See, e.g., Dyson Hague "The future of evangelical churchmanship in Canada," *The Canadian Churchman*, November 13, 1913, p. 734.

21. *The Berean*, January 29, 1846.

22. Bishop's (handwritten) letter in DOA, dated May2, 1867.

23. I can find no record of exactly *which* rubrics St James' was supposed to be flouting.

24. Anderson, p.51.

25. Anderson, p. 52.

26. *A Chronological . . .* p. 38.

27. Margaret Cohoe, p. 62.

28. This dispute, like others mentioned here, was echoed elsewhere in the 1860s and 1870s. In 1871 in Toronto, for instance, evangelicals almost won the right of local congregations to nominate their own clergy. See J.W. Grant, *The Church in the Canadian Era*, Burlington: Welch, 1988, p. 78.

29. See Robert Merrill Black, "Stablished in the faith: The Church of England in Upper Canada 1780-1867" in Alan Hayes *By Grace Co-workers*, Toronto: Anglican Book Centre, 1989, p. 38.

30. David Bebbington, *Evangelicalism in Modern Britain*, Unwin-Hyman, 1989, chapter 1.

31. John Wolffe, "Anti-Catholicism and evangelical identity in Britain the United States 1830–1860", in Mark Noll, David Bebbington and George Rawlyk, eds. *Evangelicalism: Comparative Studies of Popular Protestantism in North America, the British Isles and Beyond, 1700–1990*, New York: Oxford University Press, 1994.

32. Anthony Jackson, "Kingston's Bible Societies 1820-1875" *Historic Kingston*, 35, January 1987, pp. 19-34.

33. *A Chronological*, p. 34.

34. *The Evangelical Churchman*, 1:14, August 17, 1876.

35. Hague, *op. cit.*

36. I do not imply by this that this evangelicalism was unambiguous. William Westfall has shown in his book, *Two Cultures*, how evangelicalism faced two ways at once, contributing to both "God's dominion" and to the modernizing thrust of "economic dominion" in Ontario.

37. Rogers had ties with Alexander Sanson at Little Trinity, Toronto, for instance, through their work with the Canadian Anti-Slavery Society. And when Thomas Savery joined the congregation as rector a link was forged with one of the oldest churches in Canada, St Paul's Halifax, also still Evangelical today.

Chapter Three

1. Alvin Armstrong, *Buckskin to Broadloom*, Kingston: Whig-Standard, 1973, p. 358.

2. Osborne and Swainson, p. 63.

3. From a Toronto collection of temperance hymns, 1863, quoted in Jenna Kennedy, *Compassionate Crusade: A Study of the St James' Kingston Temperance Society, 1875–1900*, Kingston: Queen's Sociology Department, 1994, p. 3.

4. John Webster Grant, *The Church in the Canadian Era*, Burlington: Welch, 1988, p. 81.

5. William Westfall, *Two Worlds: The Protestant Culture of Nineteenth Century Ontario*, Montreal

and Kingston: McGill-Queen's University Press, 1989, p. 6.

6. Westfall, p. 187, 205.

7. Osborne and Swainson, pp. 140-142.

8. Patricia Malcolmson in Gerald Tulchinsky (ed.), *To Preserve and to Defend: Essays on Kingston in the Nineteenth Century*, Montreal and London: McGill-Queen's University Press, 1976.

9. Quoted in *The Berean*, 5:47, February 15 1849.

10. *Home Words*, May 1880, quoted in Kennedy, *Compassionate Crusade*, p. 8.

11. Jas. P. Sheraton, "The Church of England Temperance Society," *The Evangelical Churchman*, 1:3, December 7, 1876, quoted in Kennedy p. 9.

12. Kennedy, p. 11.

13. *Home Words*, November 1890, February 1891.

14. *Home Words*, May 1880.

15. *Constitution of the Kingston Temperance Society and Bylaws*, Kingston: T.H. Bentley, 1840, p. 3, quoted in Kennedy, p. 17.

16. *Home Words*, March 1879.

17. *British Whig*, 15 January 1881, p. 3, quoted Kennedy p. 26.

18. Ruth Elizabeth Spence, *Prohibition in Canada*, Toronto: The Ontario Branch of the Dominion Alliance, p. 77, quoted in Kennedy p. 23.

19. *Synod Journal*, 1910, p. 96, quoted in Kennedy p. 27.

20. See Richard Allen, *The Social Passion: Religion and Social Reform in Canada, 1914-1928*, Toronto: University of Toronto Press, 1971. Allen says that radicals (at the other end of the spectrum from conservatives) would see society organically. "Evil was so endemic and pervasive in the social order that there could be no personal salvation without social salvation" (p. 17). "Progressives" in the centre picked up elements of each in "a broad ameliorative programme of reform."

21. Dyson Hague, "The future of evangelical churchmanship in Canada," *The Canadian Churchman*, November 13 1913, p. 734.

22. Allen, p. 10.

23. *Synod Journal*, 1911, p. 72.

24. *Synod Journal*, 1914, p. 43.

25. *In Memoriam*, 1885, p.3.

26. *Home Words*, September 1895.

27. Osborne and Swainson, p. 271.

28. *In Memoriam*, p. 29.

29. *Home Words*, July 1877.

30. *Home Words*, July 1879.

31. See *In Memoriam*.

32. *In Memoriam*.

33. *In Memoriam*, p. 5.

Chapter Four

1. Robertson Davies, *Fifth Business*, Markham: Penguin, 1977 p. 14.

2. *Home Words*, October 1887.

3. John Ker McMorine, Edward J.B. Pense, R.V. Rogers, Shore Loynes and Wilson

4. 1945 Anniversary Booklet, p. 6.

5. George Comer's diary, in the possession of Mrs Betty White, Kingston.

6. *Home Words,* May 1892.

7. Quoted in 1945 Anniversary Booklet, p. 8.

8. *Home Words,* July 1909.

9. *Home Words,* November 1902.

10. *Home Words,* February 1903.

11. *Home Words,* July 1888.

12. *Home Words,* July 1996.

13. *Home Words,* July 1890.

14. Statistics from *Home Words,* May 1900. Up to 50 children came from the Orphan's Home according to *Home Words,* September 1901. A plaque on the John Deutsch University Centre, the site of the Orphan Home, commemorates the Orphan's Home and Widow's Friend Society's 125th Anniversary in 1983.

15. *Home Words,* February 1900.

16. Ellis spoke at a conference for this purpose, for example, in the summer of 1902 (*Home Words,* August).

17. *Home Words,* October 1891.

18. *Home Words,* May 1909.

19. *Home Words,* June 1898. Other military echoes included the Boy and Girl Scouts, at St James' from the Great War onwards.

20. Mentioned in Synod Committee Report, 8:11, 1911.

21. This paragraph leans heavily on Osborne and Swainson, p. 213–215.

22. Quoted Osborne and Swainson, p. 208.

23. *Home Words,* September 1895.

24. John Webster Grant, *A Profusion of Spires: Religion in Nineteenth Century Ontario,* Toronto: University of Toronto Press, 1988, p. 190.

25. Rev I.G. Shearer, a member of the Lord's Day Alliance, spoke at St James' in June 1906, for instance (*Home Words*).

26. The *Whig* report is quoted in George Dillon and William Thomson, *Kingston Portsmouth and Cataraqui Electric Railway: A History of the Limestone City's Street Car System,* Kingston: The Kingston Division of the Canadian Railroad Historical Association, 1994, p. 9.

27. *Home Words,* December 1902.

28. Pense is quoted in Douglas Fetherling, *A Little Bit of Thunder: The Strange Inner-Life of the Kingston Whig-Standard,* Don Mills: Stoddart, 1993, p. 142.

29. In the last years of his life (after 1902) Edward Pense appears to have attended St George's, for reasons I have been unable to determine. He also gave very generously to St Mark's, Barriefield in this later period.

30. Details of the Meneely Company from the Renselaer County Historical Society, 59 Second Street, Troy, New York 12180.

31. Hilda Neatby, *Queen's University, Volume 1: 1843–1917,* Montreal and Kingston: McGill-Queen's University Press, 1978, p. 238, 275.

32. Neatby, p. 238.

33. Neatby, p. 235.

34. Neatby, p. 235.

35. *Dominion Churchman,* 11:14, April 2 1885, p. 219.

36. The law faculty closed in 1864, and reopened in 1888 when Queen's appointed eight local barristers as professors. Rogers, who was one of

them, would later will his Barrie Street home to Queen's. See D.D. Calvin, *Queen's University at Kingston*, Kingston: Trustees of the University, 1941, pp. 163, 200.

37. Letter to Adam Shortt, Rogers collection, QUA. See also Neatby, p. 216.

38. *Home Words*, December 1899.

39. *Home Words*, August 1898.

40. 1945 booklet p. 11 and semi-centennial festival leaflet.

41. 1945 booklet, p. 11.

42. Unless stated otherwise, life details are found in Edna G. Ross, *John Kerr McMorine, 1842-1912: Clergyman and Botanist*, Queen's, Lorne Pierce Collection, 1969.

43. Perhaps Edith Meyer of Quebec City, whom he married in 1868, was an Anglican.

44. McMorine's starting salary at St James' was set at $1200.00 per annum plus the parsonage, *Dominion Churchman*, 11:10, March 5 1885, p. 150.

45. The other children were Julia, who married John Coleman, another Kingston clergyman, William and Arthur, who both became ministers, Agnes (?Mrs F. Ransom), Mildred and Edith (?Mrs Alex McPhail).

46. *Home Words*, December 1912.

47. Letter from R.V. Rogers to McMorine, Queen's Archives, AARCH 2269.

48. The *Parish Magazine* states that "shortly before the evening service a message was received . . ." so telegraph or telephone must have been used for a same-day communication of McMorine's death.

Chapter Five

1. Ainger (1841-1919), hymn quoted E.R. Pascoe, *Two Hundred Years of the SPG*, London: SPG, 1901.

2. *Home Words*, October 1889, October 1886.

3 See Phyllis Airhart, "Ordering a new nation and reordering Protestantism," in George Rawlyk (ed.) *The Canadian Protestant Experience*, Burlington: Welch, 1990, p. 128.

4. Alan Hayes, *Holding Forth the Word of Life: Little Trinity Church 1842-1992*, Toronto: Little Trinity, 1992, p. 23.

5. David Hempton and Myrtle Hill, *Evangelical Protestantism in Ulster Society, 1740-1890*, London and New York: Routledge, 1992, p. 129. See also Sharon Anne Cook, *Through Sunshine and Shadow: The Women's Christian Temperance Union: Evangelicalism and Reform in Ontario, 1874-1930*, Montreal and Kingston: McGill-Queen's University Press, 1995.

6. *Home Words*, December 1894, e.g.

7. O'Meara was the father of Thomas O'Meara who became rector of Little Trinity and from time-to-time preached at St James'.

8. John Webster Grant, *Moon of Wintertime: Missionaries and the Indians of Canada in Encounter since 1534*, Toronto: University of Toronto Press, 1988, p. 79.

9. Mrs G.C. Platt, *The Story of the Woman's Auxiliary in the Diocese of Ontario: "She hath done what she could" 1885-1961*, p. 240.

10. *Home Words*, October 1887.

11. Grant *Moon*, p. 187.

12. Grant *Moon*, pp. 191-196.

13. Charles Hendry, *Beyond Traplines*, Toronto: Anglican Church of Canada, 1969.

14. Missionary giving would rise to around 20% of the budget by the 1950s. But calculating these figures is very difficult, with other changes that take place, such as the proportion required for the diocese and for repairs to the building.

15. A. Hamish Ion, "Ambassadors of the Cross: Canadian Missionaries in Japan" in John Schultz and Kimitada Miwa, *Canada and Japan in the Twentieth Century*, Toronto: Oxford University Press, 1991.

16. According to E.R. Pascoe, *Two Hundred Years of the SPG*, p. 175, Waller was an SPG missionary. But John Webster Grant, in *The Church in the Canadian Era*, p. 56, says he was with the DFMS. Waller visited St James' in 1899 according to the *Home Words* report.

17. *Parish Magazine*, August 1930. The bequest was named for E.R. Welch, a churchwarden 1867-68.

18. The Deaconess and Missionary Training House is today the Centre for Christian Studies at Wycliffe.

19. *Handbook of the Women's Auxiliary of the Church of England in Canada*, p. 1.

20. *ibid*, p. 5.

21. Mrs G.C. Platt, *The Story of the Woman's Auxiliary in the Diocese of Ontario: "She hath done what she could" 1885–1961*, p. 17.

22. *ibid*, p. 19.

23. Information from Thomas Savery's daughter Barbara Minard, Halifax NS and Margaret French, Pointe Claire, PQ, August 1994.

24. *The Queen's Review*, May 1929, p. 166.

Chapter Six

1. George Grant, in a letter to his mother dated January 12, 1942, quoted in William Christian (ed.), *George Grant: A Biography*, Toronto: University of Toronto Press, 1993, p. 85.

2. Wright in George Rawlyk, ed. *The Canadian Protestant Experience*, Burlington: Welch, 1988.

3. Rod Alexander was born August 25, 1901. This story was given to Harry Juby, his neighbour, in February 1995.

4. From the note to her uncle, Mr H.A. Dupuy of Brockville, recorded in the Council Minutes for November 19, 1928, DOA Box 4-KM-11.

5. Armstrong, p. 380.

6. The donor was apparently a Mrs R.W. Leonard from St Catherines, an ex-member of St James. Centenary booklet, 1945, p. 18.

7. Reminiscences of Howard Campbell (January 1995), who grew up at St James', joining the choir when he was nine years old, in 1936.

8. For example, Queen's is the only Canadian university still to employ a chaplain.

9. *Parish Magazine*, August 1930.

10. *Parish Magazine*, April 1929; compare John Stackhouse, *Canadian Evangelicalism in the Twentieth Century*, Toronto: University of Toronto Press, 1993, chapter 5.

11. Quoted in Melvin Donald, *A Spreading Tree*, Toronto: IVCF, 1991, p. 83.

12. See Gladys and Keith Hunt, *For Christ and the University*, Downers Grove: IVP, 1991. While St James' is not named here, circumstantial evidence (the fact that Guinness had visited there before, plus the proximity of the building

to campus) is overwhelming.

13. Records of Professor John MacKenzie-Naughton held at Wycliffe College also reveal an ambivalence over his name.

14. Advisory Board Minutes, March 12 1945, 1939.

15. *Parish Magazine*, vol. 54, November 1931.

16. *ibid.* On the theme of evangelicalism and education, see also Michael Gauvreau, *The Evangelical Century: College and Creed in English Canada from the Great Revival to the Great Depression*, Montreal and Toronto: McGill-Queen's University Press, 1991.

17. The idea that the congregation swelled is assumed from the growth in total population of St James', which reached a pre-war peak of about 1,200 as Dr Naughton began his ministry in the early 1930s. Also the Sunday School had more than 300 between 1915 and 1930. See Appendix I.

18. Reginald Savery was the son of Thomas Savery by his first wife.

19. See Frank Moritsugu, "Special friend of the nikkei given praise," *Nikkei Voice*, July 1990, p. 7. Reginald Savery died in 1993.

20. Interview with Irene Cleland, April 12, 1994.

21. Dr Naughton was a member of the Queen's branch of the Masonic Lodge, with very strong imperial interests. Interview with Irene Cleland, April 12, 1994.

22. *Parish Magazine*, September, October, 1939.

23. *St James' Church Centenary, 1845-1945*, p. 18.

24. *The Canadian Churchman*, April 10 1919, p. 239.

25. *Parish Magazine*, vol. 54, February 1931.

26. See J.D. MacKenzie-Naughton, *The Princess of Wales' Own Regiment*, Kingston.

27. Margaret Angus is the source of this reminiscence.

28. Several of these stories come from the reminiscences of Margot McCurdy, during a visit to Bea Corbett in the winter of 1994. The documents are included in the St James' archive.

29. Interview September 17, 1993, Christie Gardens, Toronto.

30. Comment from Jack Grenville, November 13, 1994. Dr Naughton died in Toronto on December 2, 1972, aged 86.

Chapter Seven

1. Johnson (1822-1882), from the hymn, "City of God."

2. Records showing addresses of parishioners include the Chancel Guild duty rota and accounts books for the 1930s and 1940s. DOA.

3. Data from Osborne and Swainson, p. 302.

4. The certificates and trophies may be seen in a display cabinet in the Rogers Room at St James' church building.

5. The gifts received were for the pulpit and choir pews, three prayer desks, two sedilias, the chancel screen, the credence table, the organ, a memorial stand and carved lettering on the pulpit (the last being a gift from the Hunts). Details from Thanksgiving service leaflet.

6. Interview with Irene Cleland, April 1994.

7. Telephone interview with Tony Capon, February 1995.

8. Neither arrangement was entirely without its difficulties, and a number of important lessons was learned, sometimes painfully, as a result.

9. Jean Boyd, Irene Cleland, Irene Lawrence, John Pike, Bill Wright, Executive Council Minutes, January 20 1969.

10. W.E. McNeil, "Link between town, gown, traced," *The Whig-Standard*, Friday October 6, 1950, p. 12.

11. Executive council minutes, December 28, 1964.

12. Letter from Joanne Park to Desmond Hunt, April 4, 1961, DOA.

13. Minutes of Executive Council of Vestry, September 16 1968.

14. Pierre Berton, *The Comfortable Pew*, Toronto: McClelland and Stewart, 1965.

15. John Webster Grant, *The Church in the Canadian era*, Burlington: Welch Publishing Company, 1988, p. 195.

16. S.D. Clark, *Church and Sect in Canada*, Toronto: University of Toronto Press, 1948

17. Desmond Hunt's brother, Leslie, was principal of Wycliffe College. They had both sat at the feet of an earlier principal of Wycliffe, Dyson Hague, a noted evangelical leader. When rector in Brockville, before World War I, Hague would come to preach at St James'.

18. From a clipping owned by Naomi Hunt.

19. Ian Rennie, in "Anglican leader a most attractive witness," *Christian Week*, September 7, 1993.

20. *The Anglican*, September 1993, p. 3.

Chapter Eight

1. Margaret Atwood, *Cats Eye*, Toronto: McClelland and Stewart, 1988, p. 207.

2. If the United Church figures give any clues about the Anglican situation, it is worth noting that Sunday School attendance halved between 1966 and 1974 in that church. See John Webster Grant, *The Church in the Canadian Era*, Burlington: Welch, 1988, p. 229.

3. David Martin's *A General Theory of Secularization* (Blackwell 1978) argues that secular conditions reflect prior religious experiences. The more complete the religious monopoly, the more decisive the eventual secularization. The Canadian evidence bears this out, in my view. Other aspects of my approach to secularization are discussed in David Lyon, *The Steeple's Shadow: On the Myths and Realities of Secularization*, London UK: SPCK 1985; Grand Rapids MI: Eerdmans, 1987.

4. Several potential pitfalls lurk here. Failing to recognise the implications of having a larger proportion of women in the workforce is one. Blaming women for "loss of community" is another.

5. This analysis is indebted to Osborne and Swainson, p. 307ff.

6. Canadian census data is quoted in Pat Armstrong and Hugh Armstrong, *The Double Ghetto: Canadian Women and their Segregated Work*, Toronto: McClelland and Stewart 1984, p. 19.

7. The last phrase, "mission to maintenance", is the one used by Harold Percy in a current Wycliffe College evangelism programme. It originates in M.M. Winter's *Mission or Maintenance: A Study in New Pastoral Structures*, London: Darton,

Longman and Todd, 1973.

8. Interview with Harry Juby, September 1994.

9. According to the report of the parish planning committee of October 1971, the diocese agreed to pay half the salary of a chaplain, with the balance to come from St James'. Apparently some trouble was experienced finding a suitable candidate.

10. Various St James' people had held recent diocesan appointments: Reginald Smails, treasurer; Lorna McDougal, chair, Investment Committee; Harold Ripley, chair, Extension Committee and later treasurer; Harry Juby, treasurer; Jack Pike, chair, Salary Committee.

11. Monseigneur Hanley and Sister Pickett preached at St James'.

12. It may be worth recording that the couple who suggested Wednesday morning communion was Ossie and Ruth Studd. Hendra *Reminiscences, 1995*.

13. Hendra *Reminiscences*.

14. Parish Planning Committee Report, December 1971.

15. Anniversary leaflet, 1970.

16. *Queen's: The first one hundred and fifty years*, Newburgh: Hedgehog Productions, 1990, p. 167.

17. The physics professor was David McLay, quoted in an interview with Gordon Hendra, January 18, 1995.

18. The *Whig-Standard*, September 28, 1970.

Chapter Nine

1. Joni Mitchell, "The Priest", from the album *Ladies of the Canyon*, Siquomb Publishing Co., 1968.

2. Quote in the *Ontario Churchman*, May 1989.

3. The Walter Light Hall was opened in 1989.

4. *ibid*. See note 2.

5. Peter Taylor, quoted in the *Queen's Journal*, December 4, 1992.

6. *ibid*.

7. From *Notes by Robert Brow on his eleven years at St James' Kingston*, 1995.

8. A key element introduced by the Brows was communion for children, a topic that has been discussed extensively — without complete agreement — at a national, General Synod level. As the Brows saw it, if baptism enrolls one in the school of Christ, then children, no less than adults, can join the range of worship activities. This was one controversial element of inclusiveness.

9. *New Bottles*, London UK: BMMF, 1966; *Religion: Origins and Ideas*, London UK: Tyndale Press, 1966; *The Church: An Organic Picture of its Life and Mission*, Grand Rapids: Eerdmans, 1968.

10. Clark H. Pinnock and Robert C. Brow, *Unbounded Love: A Good News Theology for the Twenty-First Century*, Downers Grove: InterVarsity Press, 1994.

Chapter Ten

1. Bruce Cockburn, "Inner City Front," True North Records, 1981. Compare Ecclesiastes 12:6.

2. St James' tower was the first Ontario gothic on Union Street. The theme was picked up in several buildings, notably the centre facade of Miller Hall with its pointed pinnacles and the imitation of St James' shuttered ecclesiastical windows. The neo-gothic persists in the Stauffer Library, where the pinnacles are now metal rods.

3. Robinson had been at the (then new) Church of the Redeemer in Kingston at the time when Desmond Hunt was at St James' and was subsequently rector of what is spiritually a sister church to St James', Little Trinity, Toronto.

4. Walker was appointed in the fall 1990.

5. Comment from Julia Graham, January 22, 1995. In May 1995 she returned to Honduras as co-leader of another student team.

6. The "Mom's Group" began in the 1980s and was disbanded in 1992 to be partially reconstituted as the "Tuesday Group."

7. This resulted from the initiative of the new bishop, Peter Mason.

8. Such an emphasis on the "vertical" dimension was also found among United Church members by Reginald Bibby in his report for the United Church of Canada, *Unitrends*, United Church and University of Lethbridge, 1994, reported in the *Globe and Mail* as "Get back to God, study says," December 10, 1994, p. A1.

9. This relates to the Bebbington typology discussed in chapter two. See also Stephen Sykes (ed.) *The Study of Anglicanism*, London: SPCK; Philadelphia: Fortress, 1989, p. 446.

10. Several leading ideas in this paragraph originate in W.S.F. Pickering, "Sociology of Anglicanism" in Stephen Sykes *op. cit.*

11. Reginald Stackhouse, "Battling recession in the churches," *The Globe and Mail*, August 21, 1992, A15.

12. Statistics Canada survey, reported in *The Globe and Mail*, June 2 1993, A1.

13. The Prayer Book Society, the Anglican Renewal Movement and Barnabas Ministries joined together in a striking act of complementary witness at John Abbott College in June. Though no record of involvement of St James' in the PBS exists, interest in its aims does. ARM was briefly represented in the mid-1980s.

14. See *Maclean's*, April 12, 1993, "Special Report: The Religion Poll," the results of a survey conducted by George Rawlyk of Queen's and the Angus Reid Group.

15. See Grace Davie, "Believing without belonging: is this the future of religion in Britain?" *Social Compass*, 37, pp. 456–69 and Grace Davie, *Religion in Britain since 1945: Believing without Belonging*, Oxford: Blackwell, 1994.

16. It so happens that these correspond roughly with Reginald Stackhouse's prescription for emphasising growth, fellowship and meeting needs. See note 10.

17. See Danièle Hervieu-Léger, *Vers un nouveau Christianisme*, Paris: Cerf, 1986, pp. 57–60, and Robert Wuthnow, *Sharing the Journey: Support Groups and America's New Quest for Community*, New York: Free Press, 1994.

18. Rather than deciding what could be done with the money available the idea is to decide first

what the church *ought* to do and then find the funds.

19. Some of the dangers are outlined in Janet Finch, *Married to the Job: Wives' Incorporation in Men's Work*, London: Allen and Unwin, 1983.

20. Although other factors are involved, periods looked back on with special warmth are ones in which church leadership was in the hands of both men and women (even if the latter were unpaid wives of clergy). The implications of this in a time when it is neither appropriate nor possible to expect women to be "married to the job" should not be lost on those making decisions about leadership.

21. I try to explain in a straightforward manner what is meant by the postmodern turn in David Lyon, *Postmodernity*, Minneapolis: University of Minnesota Press, 1994.

22. The question is well addressed by Alister McGrath in *The Renewal of Anglicanism*, Harrisburg PA: Morehouse Publishing, 1993.

23. Marguerite Van Die reminds us that a task of history is to connect memory with hope. "Earlier Generations Teach Contemporary Lessons," *Christian Week*, June 8, 1993, p. 13.